THE THREE CROWNS OF FLORENCE

THE
THREE CROWNS
OF FLORENCE

Humanist Assessments of
Dante, Petrarca and Boccaccio

Edited and Translated by
David Thompson and Alan F. Nagel

Harper & Row, Publishers
New York, Evanston, San Francisco, London

For Damon Illeo
Sine quo non

LIBRARY OF CONGRESS CATALOG NUMBER: 76–172502

STANDARD BOOK NUMBER: 06–139525–0

CONTENTS

PREFACE

To illustrate the thought and literature of Italian Humanism, we have focused on a question of considerable interest to recent historians: How did the humanists assess the "Three Crowns of Florence," Dante, Petrarca and Boccaccio? Our texts represent most of the humanists' favorite forms, and several themes dear to successive generations of writers (for example, the relation between Latin and Italian; the relative merits of the active and of the contemplative life). Beyond a necessary minimum of annotation, we have allowed the authors to speak for themselves.

Very little of this material has previously appeared in English. Mr. Thompson has been primarily responsible for the Introduction, Bruni's *Dialogues,* Manetti, Poliziano, Ficino, Verino and Pico; Mr. Nagel for Filelfo, Bruni's *Lives,* Palmieri, Landino, Lorenzo and Bembo. Our work was facilitated by a semester's leave of absence granted Mr. Thompson by the University of New Mexico in the spring of 1969, and by a Fulbright fellowship awarded Mr. Nagel for the academic year 1968–69. For assistance at various points we thank Professor James Hutton of Cornell University, Professor Sergio Baldi of the University of Florence and the staff of the Biblioteca Nazionale in Florence. We are particularly grateful to Professor Eugenio Garin, to the Casa Editrice A. Morano and to Professor Pietro Piovani (director of the Collana di Filosofia) for permission to translate the introductory essay.

Introduction

DANTE IN THE RENAISSANCE*

Eugenio Garin

The great century of Humanism opened with a famous
polemic between ancients and moderns, Niccoli's harsh censure and Bruni's calm reply [*No. 3*]. The prominence of this
polemic and other, sixteenth-century, literary controversies
has obscured—and perhaps it was legitimate—other aspects of
Dante's various fortunes in the age of the so-called Renaissance. The observations which follow aim only at contribut-
ing to the determination of Dante's presence in Italian culture—especially Florentine and Tuscan—between the end
of the Trecento and the beginning of the Cinquecento: in
the time, that is, of the "rebirth of letters."

To start with we should ask: Where did the humanists
place Dante, when they fixed the temporal limits of that
renewal of which they very clearly felt themselves the arti-
ficers and protagonists? When they divided history into periods, which they did consciously, did they include Dante or
exclude him from the movement they had programmed and

* "Dante nel Rinascimento," published originally in *Rinascimento*, Rivista dell' Istituto Nazionale di Studi sul Rinascimento, Second series, Vol.
VII (1967); and then (with a few slight changes) in Garin's *L'età Nuova:
Ricerche di storia della cultura dal XII al XVI secolo*, Collana di
Filosofia, XI (© Copyright 1969 by Casa Editrice A. Morano, Naples). I have
omitted two introductory paragraphs, the author's notes and a brief appendix
on Salutati as a translator of Dante—Translator's note.

put into effect? In general, the texts agree most on two names: by common consensus, Francesco Petrarca and Manuel Chrysoloras close the barbarous age and open the new, the former restoring classical Latin, the latter reintroducing acquaintance with the Greek world. A justly famous page of Leonardo Bruni places the end of the medieval night, which lasted seven hundred years, at the beginning of the Byzantine master's courses in Florence.

However, the periodization is then variously articulated and vanishes, precisely apropos of Dante. Proceeding in reverse—that is, from the end of the Quattrocento and from the court of Lorenzo the Magnificent, with its renewed Dantean fervor—it is not difficult to go back to Boccaccio along the succession of themes converging in the exaltation of Dante, the resurrector of poetry, who revived it from darkness to light. In 1372 Boccaccio writes to Jacopo Pizzinga of Messina, protonotary of King Federigo IV, that Dante had been the first to return to the source "neglected for many centuries." Domenico di Bandino fixes a date, and a very significant one: the twelfth century and the *Anticlaudianus* of Alanus de Insulis. After Alanus poetry was dead, at least great theological poetry; with Dante poetic theology was brought back to life: "After the *Anticlaudianus* . . . poetry had been abandoned; Dante led it forth to the light." Filippo Villani reproduces the motif, but with a leap back concerning the beginning of the dark ages; he accepts approximately the sort of periodization that will spread through the whole Quattrocento. The dark interval, the night of knowledge, begins with the decline of the Western empire: not Alanus de Insulis and the *Anticlaudianus,* but Claudian and the guilt and avarice of the Caesars: "after Claudian . . . when poetry lay uncultivated, unadorned . . . he rescued it as if from an abyss of darkness and called it back into the light, and giving his hand raised it from a prostrate position onto its feet." The two texts, of Villani and of Bandino, are parallel and correspond to each other: they declare a not casual interdependence, except for that time difference, which is considerable and—if the reading "after the *Anticlaudianus*" should be kept—extremely significant. (However, it is hardly surprising in a friend of that Salutati who had often looked to the "renaissance" of the twelfth century. The comparison Alanus-Dante would not necessarily appear scandalous to Salutati: he had a high regard for Alanus the poet-theologian, and was not unaware even of Alanus' commentary on the *Rhetorica ad Herennium,* which he made use of and diffused.) On the other hand, how not underline the force of the differences in texts that are parallel and in some respects identical? In Domenico di Bandino, a penetrating historical judgment implied a series of consequences: comparison of the *Commedia* to the philosophic-theological poems of the twelfth century; Dante's close connection with the medieval age; detailed polemic against the "moderns," destroyers of poetry, from the thirteenth to the beginning of the fourteenth century. In Filippo Villani, the shift in the beginning of the darkness to the crisis of the Roman Empire; the extension of the duration of the dark centuries from the fifth to the end of the thirteenth; the total condemnation of nine centuries of barbarism—all this indicates that the myth of the Renaissance has been born. In it Dante has the position of initiator.

Again at Florence, about a century later, at the court of Lorenzo, Paolo Cortesi, in his dialogue *On Learned Men,* presents a panorama of contemporary literature. Searching for its roots, he comes to discuss the placement of the beginning of the new times—so far as they are characterized by a return to the ancients—in Chrysoloras and his Florentine school. Immediately he is presented with the problem of Dante and Petrarca, of Boccaccio, of Giovanni da Ravenna (il Conversino), of Coluccio Salutati, all united in a single group. "I should never," he observes, "dare deny Dante and Petrarca an ardent love for antiquity. Unfortunately, the same thing happens with Dante as with an ancient painting: the colors having vanished, only the outlines please us." This important judgment is followed by lofty praise of the *Commedia,* along with the lament that Dante's Latin is not equal to his vernacular ("would that he had been able to commit his thoughts to Latin as well as he rendered illustrious his native language!"). Petrarca, however—and this is important towards the end of the Quattrocento—is judged no differently. His Latin is bad ("his language is not Latin, and much too unpolished"), although the vernacular lyrics show genius ("if the beauty and splendor of the Latin language had been present"). Certainly it was Petrarca who with his enthusiasm brought the study of eloquence back into the light; unfortunately, since he was born "in the dregs of all centuries," his work stands revealed, finally, as a medicine which is salutary, not pleasant ("for the sake not of sweetness but of health"). Boccaccio's Latin is poorly composed, "contaminated by utterly improper usage," while the language of Giovanni da Ravenna and of Salutati is harsh and dreary: "never . . . were they able to keep from harshness and dejection."

For Cortesi the effective beginning of the new literature is placed at the point where a revived knowledge of classical Latin meets the study of Greek: the renewal occurs at the convergence of the two great ancient literatures, with a decisive weight given to Greek. Unless (and this is to be underlined) Dante is not just joined to Petrarca, to Giovanni da Ravenna and to Salutati—as scholars all, enthusiasts of antiquity and hence furtherers and forerunners of the renewal—but is simply, because of his vernacular works, placed by himself, in an eminent position, first in substance if not in form.

Cortesi, the Ciceronian, who against Poliziano defended imitation to the bitter end, dedicated his dialogue to Lorenzo in 1490. Some decades earlier an illustrious jurist, Benedetto Accolti, chancellor of the Republic, had dedicated to Cosimo a more interesting text, the dialogue *On the Pre-eminence of the Men of His Own Age,* a sort of incunabulum of the *querelle* between ancients and moderns. For Accolti, Dante is "modern," like Petrarca: both restorers of ancient "culture" against Gothic barbarism. Their perfect Florentine vernacular stands to Latin in the relation Latin stands to Greek; neither of the two can be placed lower than Homer or Virgil, not even on formal, linguistic grounds. Both sovereign poets in the vernacular, both were very skillful Latin writers: "they were, however, very skillful and learned, not at all unfitted for Latin poetry."

For all the difference between the situation at the time of Cosimo and that established with Lorenzo, in the enthusiastic elaboration of the myth of Florence (which seeks its own Homer in Dante and its own Virgil in Petrarca), Accolti agrees with Cortesi in exalting Dante's poetry and placing him within the period to which the one and the other feel they belong. Moreover, with his pictorial comparison Cortesi solicits the analogy with Giotto, whose greatness Poliziano was singing at about that time. When confronted with analogous problems, Vasari—who was so successful in periodizing the rebirth of the arts—will distinguish between "ancient" and "old," between classical and "Byzantine" Greece, in a symmetrical correspondence of Gothic barbarism and Greek barbarism. Giotto, like Dante, is "ancient," not "old," and hence truly "modern," that is, truly contemporary. At the same time, as Florence, in the elaboration of her myth, was celebrated as the daughter of Rome, or a new Athens—or, with Savonarola, a new Jerusalem—so her greatest poet's Homeric majesty was emphasized, or his links with Virgil, or his prophetic inspiration. But Dante remained, for Florence, the great "modern" poet.

In this connection one insists on a term which, between Middle Ages and Renaissance, was often used with precise—if often diverse—polemic values. "If we consider the modern poets," says Accolti, and he means Dante, Petrarca and all the protagonists of the return to the ancients. About a century earlier, the placement of Dante among the "moderns"— whether to praise or to savage him—meant exactly the opposite: "moderns," in the arts, were the "Goths" and "Byzantines"; in philosophy, the English logicians or the scientists of Paris, against whose frayed subtleties the return to the classical tradition was posed as a human redemption. Between the end of the Trecento and the beginning of the Quattrocento—truly on a contested border, to use Gilson's term—to set Dante among the "moderns" meant, for friends and foes, to put him in the orbit of Scholasticism, among those "scientists" and "logicians" who, in the very same Scholasticism, had combatted the classical authors and destroyed the great theological poetry of the twelfth century, like that of Alanus de Insulis. For Cino Rinuccini, who was exalting him, as for Niccoli who was destroying him, the "modernness" of Dante had fundamentally the same meaning: his having no part in the return of the ancients, and, vice versa, his inclusion in late medieval scholastic culture, logical and scientific, which in fact had been completely foreign to Dante. At the moment when they clash most vividly, the humanist avant-gardes (as Dionisotti would say) and the most arrogant scholastics, nominalists and scientists seem completely in agreement in wishing to expunge Dante's name from the culture of the "rebirth of letters." Dante is like Occam, whether for Francesco Landini or Niccolò Niccoli. Not so for Salutati, or for Bruni, or for Filelfo. And what then?—What is the real substance of the famous polemic against Dante at the beginning of the Quattrocento, which seems to shatter the unanimous consensus with which the humanists include him in the cultural renewal and consider him one of their own? Apropos of Dante, is there really a contrast so striking and widespread as there is said to be, between an enthusiastic Trecento and an iconoclastic early Quattrocento, which then immediately witnesses an uninterrupted recovery until the end of the century and the neoplatonic transformation of Lorenzo's circle?

The answer calls for a critical re-examination of the situation between the close of the fourteenth century and the beginning of the fifteenth: an examination to be conducted with some independence as regards Alexander Wesselofsky—and, still later, Lorenzo Mehus. Although they are remote from us by one and two centuries, their results, considered undisputed, have fixed models and reference points which have not been contested or ever seriously altered or appreciably increased.

Once more a valuable point of reference is presented by Salutati, who, offering himself as executor of the humanist program of Petrarca and Boccaccio, contributed strongly to Chrysoloras' coming, exercising a decisive influence on Bruni and on his friends. It is customary to recall that even Salutati regretted that the *Commedia* had not been composed in Latin; but that lament is not analyzed. Nor is the maturing of an evaluation which was not always the same in the course of years followed in its nuances. Salutati says if Dante had attained in Latin the perfection he achieved in his mother tongue, he would have surpassed Homer and Virgil together. Nothing is more profound, more elegant, more learned than the *Commedia:* in it, "like stars in the firmament," are all the sciences, philosophy, theology, history, customs, laws [*No.* 2]. Even from the formal point of view, Dante has attained a unique perfection: "there rhetorical figures of thought and language are evident in such splendor that you would be hard put to find such great embellishments elsewhere, even in the greatest authors." Only once does Salutati allude to a superiority of Petrarca's, but on an exceptional occasion: in the letter of August 16, 1374, to Roberto Guidi of Battifolle, on the poet's death [*No.* 1]. And his friend Benvenuto da Imola contradicted him: Petrarca, perhaps, was "the greater orator"; Dante, certainly, "the greater poet." Then, at the end of his life (March 26, 1406), writing to Poggio Bracciolini, precisely in comparing the two authors so dear to him Salutati seems to place the poetry of the *Commedia* in a position by itself, beyond comparisons. And already in June of 1383, when criticizing the lowly style and monkish *cursus* of Benvenuto's commentary, he had exalted the extraordinary loftiness of Dante's poetry.

There is more: Salutati finds in Dante his own political ideals and his own theological-metaphysical conceptions. One thinks of the *De tyranno,* with its approval of the condemnation of Brutus and Cassius, and its defense of Caesar—so singular in Salutati, a valiant defender of *Florentina libertas.* One thinks of the violent polemic against Cecco d'Ascoli, in the final part of the *De fato, fortuna et casu.* These last are pages worthy of more attention than they usually receive, for a special prominence of theirs which is threefold: for the enucleation of a Dantesque theory of determinism and astrology, drawn from the passages on fortune (in *Inferno,* VII and *Purgatorio,* XVI); for some fifty hexameters in which Salutati tries a Latin translation of Dante's terzine; and for an unreserved judgment on both the language and content of the poem. The hexameters ought to be reread. "Rashly but faithfully," says Salutati, confessing their distance from the majestic Dantesque solemnity that has found in the Florentine vernacular the most perfect expressive medium in the world: "the polished idiom of the Florentines, which alone and beyond all the world's tongues answers to rhythmic songs with elegance and sweetness." To his praise of the language, to a subtle analysis of the difficulty of translating from Latin into the vernacular and from the vernacular into Latin, Salutati adds a characterization of Dante's art, whose "majesty" derives from the converging in it of all the sciences ("not except by a concourse of all the sciences is it accomplished") placed together under the sign of the two luminaries, philosophy and theology, to represent the mystery of man's life between sin and redemption. The old chancellor's position has an exemplary value: Dante belongs, like Petrarca, to the new culture; his poetry is set on an exceptional plane, liberating the vernacular to be a language of art and of thought. His work expresses all the mystery of life and stands beside that of Homer and Virgil. Not only is it full, extraordinarily full, of the paradigmatic value of antiquity; linked consciously with the great classics, it attains like them the status of an ideal model. If Salutati had divided history into periods, as Bruni did, he would have put Dante within the confines of the renewed culture, for his exceptional awareness of antiquity, for his being in his own turn truly a "classic": not imitation, but to be imitated.

In such fashion Dante was entering undisputed within the age when letters were being reborn, in a symmetrical correspondence between the *Commedia* and the poems of Homer and Virgil. Picking up where his friend Coluccio left off, Leonardo Bruni will say: "Writing in literary or vernacular style has nothing to do with the case, any more than the difference between writing in Greek or in Latin" [*No. 5*]. Dante's Florentine is to Virgil's Latin as Virgil's Latin is to Homer's Greek. Giannozzo Manetti will not only make the statement his own and amplify it, but will insert Dante within the picture of the "rebirth," to the extent of applying to him for poetry the *topos* of a resurrection from darkness to light after nine centuries (a *topos* used for the return of Cicero with Petrarca, of Greek with Chrysoloras, of painting with Giotto, of architecture with Brunelleschi) . "This great poet," Giannozzo writes, "first brought poetry back into the light after it had been dead, or asleep, for some nine hundred years. When it lay prostrate he so raised it up that by his merit it seemed recalled from exile, and recalled to light from the darkness in which it had remained completely lifeless for so many years." Filippo Villani's beginning is enriched; it will become a "national" commonplace; and we shall find it again in the oration on the death of Lorenzo, spoken in Naples in 1492 by the Milanese Aurelio Bienato (transplanted there about 1465, teacher at the university, and from 1485 bishop of Martorano).

Salutati had maintained unreservedly that Dante was a "classic," from both the formal, "rhetorical" point of view and from the point of view of content—"moral," philosophic, theological. For him Dante was worthy of being counted among the "authors" that the teachers of grammar and rhetoric "read" publicly. This valuation is sanctioned by the reading of Dante that the officers of the University of Florence will entrust generally to teachers of rhetoric—but not only to them—bound, on official holidays, to add commentary upon Dante to that on the "major authors." Dante will be "read" publicly even elsewhere, in the Trecento and Quattrocento: by Benvenuto da Imola, perhaps even before 1373, at Bologna; from May, 1396, onward, at Siena, and for almost fifty years, by Giovanni di Ser Buccio da Spoleto, a humble teacher of grammar and rhetoric; at intervals, and in various forms, at Città di Castello, at Ferrara, at Milan, at Verona. The Florentine reading, however, was another thing: at the university, with regular "policies"; and it is worthwhile to take notice of its variations and its from time to time diverse significance.

Dante is read in 1381 by Antonio, a parish priest of Vado, to whom Francesco Landini (il Cieco degli Organi) addresses his biting defense of Occam against the grammarians, that

is, his exaltation of the "barbarous Britons" against the
supporters of classical tendencies. But the priest of Vado is
also the grammarian chosen as companion of Domenico di
Bandino, who wishes to comment upon Seneca in competi-
tion with him, and for this draws upon himself the criticism
of Salutati. In the first decades of the Quattrocento we several
times find Giovanni Malpaghini da Ravenna retained to read
rhetoric, the "major authors" and "especially also the book of
Dante, to be read on holidays"; and then Giovanni Gherardo
da Prato: "to read on any holiday the book, commonly called
il Dante, of the illustrious and famous poet Dante Alighieri
of Florence, and the moral songs of this very Dante, written
and composed by Dante himself." Francesco Filelfo [*No.* 4]
will read Dante in 1431, in Santa Maria del Fiore; and it will
be no accident if around that course there gathers the strife,
exquisitely political, between adherents of Marsuppini (the
Mediceans), and adversaries of "tyranny," supporters of
Filelfo. Dante becomes the banner of the anti-Medicean
party, of Rinaldo degli Albizi and Palla di Nofri Strozzi;
while over against them, with Marsuppini, stands Niccoli—
the fierce critic of Dante and the great men of the Trecanto—
who after some thirty years still sings the old song: "the
reading of this divine poet," Filelfo replies from the cathedral, "whom my ignorant rivals call reading matter for cobblers and bakers."

Dante and the *Nicomachean Ethics,* in other words, the
texts always dear to the "republicans," are the center of
Filelfo's readings, which become a civic event. "He continually had two hundred pupils and more; he made . . . many
young men learned in Latin and in Greek. . . . And to
gratify the appetites for letters, they induced him to read
Dante in Santa Liperata, on holidays. To train his pupils
. . . he made each one compose an oration in the vernacular
[on Dante], and he used to read publicly in Santa Liperata,

in the pulpit. . . ." From December 24, 1431, dates the resolution which approves Filelfo's "carrying a chair and placing it in the Church of Santa Maria del Fiore, or elsewhere, as it may please the said master Francesco Filelfo, for the reading of Dante." His adversaries, that is the Mediceans, and Marsuppini and Niccoli, incited riots. It is known, says the resolution, "that there are some who against injunctions and deliberations . . . and honor and good character, have boasted and do boast that they will assail and occupy the aforesaid school and chair, or keep master Francesco himself from reading. . . ." It is a sad story of academic rivalries and professorial jealousies, of provocateurs and suborned students, until the attack of May, 1433, in which Filelfo is wounded with a knife (his face disfigured forever) and forced to repair to Siena.

The affair of Filelfo, consigned to precise documents—with Dante's name at the center, and in the background not only Niccoli, Bruni and Marsuppini, but Rinaldo degli Albizi, Palla Strozzi, Cosimo and the whole Medicean party—stands there to bear witness how risky it is to judge sharp polemics and university conflicts only in literary terms, leaving profound political collisions out of consideration. At the time of Salutati and Bruni, or of Filelfo and Marsuppini—as later at the time of Landino and Benivieni—the distinctive mark of the Dante controversy is not stylistic or linguistic, but political; or rather, as always, the cultural fact is indissolubly connected with graver vicissitudes. Rhetoric, certainly, that of Filelfo; and, earlier, that of Salutati and Bruni; and, afterwards, that of Nesi or Benivieni. But Palla Strozzi's exile is not rhetoric; nor are Filelfo's knife wounds; nor, later, are the killings by mob violence, or the fires burning men at the stake. By cutting that tie between rhetoric and politics, between literary facts (of language and style) and "moral" content, one risks speaking to little effect—as a critic of the stature of Vittorio Rossi used to do—of the Dante "stupidities" of Poggio and Salutati, letting the real dimensions of the literary facts themselves pass unnoticed.

However, to return to the readers of Dante at the University of Florence, it is worthy of note that after Antonio d'Arezzo and Lorenzo Pisano, canon of San Lorenzo, already in 1439 we find the holiday Dante commentary combined not with rhetoric and ethics but with theology, first in the Dominican Fra Girolamo di Giovanni, of Santa Maria Novella; then, around 1470, in Fra Domenico di Giovanni, also a Dominican, who reads theology "and the work of Dante, the Florentine poet." But discussion on Dante at the time of Lorenzo, Ficino, Landino, Botticelli, Benivieni and Savonarola is completely different—like Lorenzo's Florence, far from that of Cosimo.

The order of our treatment takes us back again, to the origin of that quip about the poet for cobblers and bakers, which Niccoli obstinately repeated from the years of Salutati to those of Filelfo, always the same and always equally spiteful and sterile. Though probably a somewhat isolated fact, and the sign of a superficial extremism, oddly enough it has cast a long shadow over the whole great century of Humanism, impairing the perspectives for an accurate appraisal of Dante's presence in the Quattrocento.

Salutati was a humanist, as was his disciple Leonardo Bruni; nevertheless, both were ardent admirers of Dante. The detractors like Niccoli were also humanists. What, then, are the lines of demarcation of the groups? Who are the protagonists of the polemic? What are the exact terms? The texts are well known, but few in number and always the same, and concentrated in the same period, in the same circle of men: at Florence, between the close of the Trecento and the beginning of the Quattrocento. And they are, be it observed, the texts in which the detractors are fought, in which response is made to the "grammarians," to the extremists who criticize the great men of the Trecento. We do not have the writings of the iconoclastic avant-garde, nor do we know that there were any such writings. There were speeches; but those of Niccoli, related in the first of Bruni's dialogues to Vergerio, are reconstructed—perhaps faithfully, but in an elegant dialectical exercise, pro and con, as was usual in the schools of rhetoric. Dante is attacked, then defended. At Santa Maria in Campo, in the school conducted by Cino di Francesco Guidetti (in 1386), was trained precisely one of the personages of Bruni's dialogues—and an illustrious personage, close to the avant-garde positions—Roberto de' Rossi. Since the notebooks of those exercises have remained for us, we know well how rhetoric (for example) was defended from one side, demolished from the other (Roberto was destroying it). Bruni's dialogues are no more than a very elegant and subtle document of this "game," with a basis certainly of historical truth, but where the virtuosity of the dialectical exercise (which, besides, is made clear) cannot be put in the shade.*

As for Niccoli, he is always the personage pinpointed at the center of the polemic, the extreme point of criticism, from the time of Salutati to that of Filelfo—always with the same invective. Antiquarian and tireless collector of texts, depicted by Vespasiano among almost D'Annunzian delicacies, in reality enamored of antiquity to the point of fanaticism, Niccoli had a slanderous and intemperate tongue, with a taste for destructive criticism. "He will declare war," wrote Bruni, "on all the great geniuses, not only those alive but even the dead." He not only despised Dante, Petrarca and Boccaccio,

---

* It is perhaps only fair to refer the reader to Hans Baron's answer to this "rhetorical hypothesis" (which Garin had advanced in 1960); see the postscript in *The Crisis of the Early Italian Renaissance* (rev. 1-vol. ed., Princeton, N.J., 1966), pp. 512–514 (note 47) —Translator's note.

but said of Saint Thomas that he had been devoid of both genius and culture. He had, according to Bruni, torn Chrysoloras to pieces, to the point of forcing him to leave Florence; he had covered Guarino with insults. "The vituperation . . . of a foul and abominable buffoon, and of an utterly absurd wretch such as you are, ought rightly to seem the highest praise," Bruni concludes. This too is an excessive polemic, but one to bear in mind, as we must bear in mind the sterility of Niccoli and his followers, whatever there were of them: "I have not yet seen appear," another defender of Dante will object, "any historical or philosophical or poetic work of theirs." Nor should the other important assertion be forgotten: "the Greek philosophers and poets would be vituperable, then, who did not have Latin, and the Latin poets and philosophers, who did not have Greek, according to the opinion of these bilinguals and trilinguals . . . [but] the former are still alive, and the latter are dead."

On the other hand, on rereading the documents—not many —of that conflict of ideas, one comes even to suspect that the central motif of that collision was in fact not Dante, nor even the Latin-vernacular relation, and that a disproportionate part has been attributed to Niccoli himself, with his orthographic-grammatical fixations. The testimony in question is, above all, Francesco Landini's poem in praise of Occam; Cino Rinuccini's invective; and, with the *Dialogues* of Bruni [*No. 3*], a few other pages in particular of Giovanni and Domenico da Prato, already submitted in evidence by Wesselofsky. They are interconnected texts, clearly bound to the same affair. Now in all of them the discussion fundamentally is not in fact on Dante: it is on the arts and sciences, on the trivium and quadrivium—above all, on the trivium: on the logic, or rather on the dialectic, of the nominalists. The names are those of Occam and Entisber; Giovanni da Prato, author of the *Paradiso degli Alberti,* will go so far as to cite

Clymenton Langley and Burleigh; Bruni will put in Niccoli's mouth the name of Ferabrich, or Richard Feribrigus. That is, here they fight for the British "sophists," for positions of the second half of the fourteenth century, foreign to Dante and violently opposed by Petrarca. Salutati himself will attack them severely, even if his interlocutors will be less "old," as befitted a man perfectly up to date. He will seek to convert to humane studies—and will say he has won him—a logician like Pietro degli Alboini da Mantova. The new logic, in Italy, was giving forth by now the great works of Paolo Veneto.

The defenders of the "moderns," of Dante, of the vernacular—or, simply, of the "three crowns"—move on a very curious platform: they fight for an antiquated "sophistic," on philosophic frontiers which are by now in every sense behind the times; and to give prestige to their own slightly worn out theses they call upon Dante, who had been completely foreign to nominalist logic, and even upon Petrarca, who had been strongly averse to it, and indeed at the vanguard in the battle against the "barbarous Britons." An attentive reading of Rinuccini's *Invettiva* ["Invective Against Certain Slanderers of Dante, Petrarca and Boccaccio"] reveals immediately that the defense of Dante, Petrarca and Boccaccio, which is prominent in the title, is on the contrary marginal in the text. It is a question of the arts, above all grammar and dialectic, and more particularly the ways of understanding them and their methods: it is, in short, about the arts of language. Rinuccini is very clear: away with grammar! The conflict has broken out between "historical" method ("they cry out . . . which grammar is better, that of the time of the comic Terence, or of the heroic Virgil") and "logical," structural method ("the signification, the distinction . . . of words, the harmony of the parts of the oration") . The "scientific and circumspect" Cino stands, obviously, for the second.

With rhetoric and dialectic the situation is analogous: on one side, the idea that it is a question of natural endowments to be trained on the great classical orators; on the other, the conviction that they are rigorous sciences. "They plot how large was the number of first-rate orators, maintaining that rhetoric is nothing, and that man has it naturally—not knowing what the fourfold exordium is, the latent insinuation, the brief, lucid narration . . . the tripartite division. . . . Nor again do they care what an accepted enthymeme is, or a demonstrative syllogism or the other parts of logic which are very useful in disputations and philosophic proofs."

This is the problem: Is a good rhetorical and dialectical training—that is to say, the art of confutation and persuasion—achieved by studying the classics and imitating ancient paradigms, or by analyzing general procedures and establishing permanent structures? "Does philosophy . . . need . . . so many languages or years, or the names of princes, empires, monarchies, cities, chronicles and similar commemorations?" Dante on one side, Niccoli on the other, are occasions and pretexts in that greater battle, sharpened from the time of Mussato onward, which involved the profound sense of the return to the "ancients," and the new study of the classics, and the way of considering language, poetry and philosophy. "Ancients" and "moderns" were only ambiguous terms, which could change parts. Beyond, more fundamental, was the polemic between the sense of history and the significance of the classics on the one hand, and logical-dialectical technical knowledge on the other: if one wishes, between two ways of understanding logic and dialectic, between two methods of instruction. Here Dante, finally, becomes a disputed divinity, or a contested authority; and all the great humanists want him with them. Not Niccoli; certainly Bruni. The *Dialogues,* however they be dated, however their relation be interpreted, are a defense of the new rhetoric, an elegant example of the new dialectic, and the vindication of Dante as symbol and tutelary divinity of the new culture.

It should not be forgotten that the greatest part of the Quattrocento's production consists of treatises, of "essays" in criticism and history, ethics and politics, where the stress ends by falling on the "contents" rather than on purely formal characteristics. Dante theologian and prophet, politician and moralist, is put forward as the type of the learned man active in the city, of the intellectual whose virtue triumphs over fortune, emblem of *Florentina libertas,* firm assertor of the continuity of the classical tradition: Virgil's pupil, Homer's rival.

If this perspective is correct, Niccoli's criticism not only does not characterize a direction, but is not even decisive for understanding the relation between Dante and a few decades of Florentine life; it is, at most, an episode of picturesque intemperance on the part of some impotent (and a bit blackguardly) scholar, of a weak-willed sham avant-garde: if a fairly recent critical study had not spoken of it so much, there would be no need to dwell much on it. Likewise because it does not serve to pinpoint the shift in the appraisal of Dante between Coluccio Salutati and the time of Palmieri, or to exclude our dealing only with a fact of language and style. Bruni's work, from the *Dialogues* to the *Life,* shows precisely how it was an ideal of life which was seeking in Dante a model or a symbol—how it was a view of the world which wished to find itself in him as in a master and guide, rejecting to the root Niccoli's thesis that the Dante question reduced itself to a literary one.

Hans Baron has very learnedly discussed the development of Bruni's thought, from the first of the *Dialogues* to the *Laudatio* on down to the *Life of Dante,* along an arc of thirty-five years from 1401 to about May, 1436. Detaching the First from the Second Dialogue, he carries the latter to August–

October, 1405, the *Laudatio* to 1403–04. On the other hand, he places Rinuccini's *Invettiva* around 1400, while carrying to 1420 that of Domenico da Prato, which would be turned also against Bruni. Baron's elegant investigation could permit a varied change of positions in Bruni himself, about Dante and the vernacular, and a more shaded periodization. If instead, as seems probable, the appearance Bruni wished to give them is restored to the two *Dialogues,* harmonizing them in a characteristic dialectical disputation, then the diverse shadings, however fully developed, are presented to us as the intended motifs of a more or less faithfully drawn conflict, of contemporary positions. This attenuates the possibility of dating with exactitude the various fortunes of the vernacular, and hence of Dante. But at the same time one perceives ever better the definition in Florence (beyond fourteenth-century "poetic" discussions) of a Dante who is symbol and expression of the city on a cultural plane, equal to Homer for Athens and Virgil for Rome. In terms of *laudatio,* Dante, having become a sign of nobility and the incarnation of an ideal, withdraws from the collision of the "sects" and wins a position by himself. If Bruni's oration against Niccoli (*In nebulonem maledicum*—"Against a Scurrilous Wretch") is from 1424, if Niccoli continues in his attacks until the time of Filelfo, if Dante's name is mixed into the conflicts between old "republicans" and Mediceans, it is still true that the operation which places him definitively as the paradigm for an age and a world—of its spiritual values, of its most original ethical-political entreaties—is already far advanced about 1430. Between the vernacular Dante orations of Filelfo and his pupils, and the *Civic Life,* there is a great distance in value but a small distance in time. Between 1432 and 1433 Palmieri sets going in full—in a vernacular which is already reaffirming and renewing itself through "grammar"—that transfiguration of the *Commedia*'s author, and of the *Com-*

media itself, which will culminate half a century later in Landino's edition and commentary, in the shadow of Lorenzo's power. Dante Platonic poet, Dante prophet, Dante emblematic expression of the *vita civile* of the Florentine citizens, of the Florentine people.

> All was light to his gentle spirit . . .
> He ennobled the vernacular
> As Virgil did Latin and Homer Greek . . .
> O everlasting life of his and happy,
> Chosen vessel, our example.

The tragic poet of Siena (a suicide, it seems, between 1419 and 1420) had given voice in his *"capitolo"* to a motif that was becoming consolidated in those years. In the proemium of his treatise [*No.* 6] Palmieri writes: "First and worthy above all others . . . In great things he always is sublime and elevated; in small things a diligent depictor of true propriety." Dante is not only a pleasing poet but "orator, philosopher and theologian," "gay, plain, jocund, and serious"; only he who has "great genius and abundant learning" will be able to overtake the significance "in his poetic veilings." As is well known, the work closes by taking up again the finale of Plato's *Republic* and the myth of Er—only that we are among the dead of Campaldino, with Dante, who after having fought "as strongly as he was able," goes around among the bodies to find "a dear companion of his." And he, "like unto one alive," through divine will reveals to Dante the "secret he had seen"—the mystery of the next world—so that Dante may make it "manifest to the human race." The "secret" is a civic ideal established in Ciceronian terms within a platonic frame: "no work among men can be better than providing for the welfare of the fatherland, preserving cities, and maintaining the union and concord of well-assembled multitudes." Those who make such contributions "will live content eternally with the other blessed." Thus he calls upon its greatest poet to show the people of Florence its mission. And let it not be forgotten that the *Civic Life* is published for the first time in Florence, in two printings of 1529, at a fearful moment. Reading the close of the book, one cannot but recall another sage so dear to these writers: Socrates at Potidea. Here Dante, in that field of the dead, having heard from his friend the commandment of God, "provided for the burial and returned to the army." No differently, in his *Life* Giannozzo Manetti will appeal several times to Socrates; and already in 1436 Bruni had with singular effectiveness designated Dante an example of the "social animal": fighter, magistrate, father of a family, sage, philosophic poet, educator of his people [*No. 5*]:

There is, then, one sort of poet through internal possession and agitation of mind; the other sort comes through knowledge and study, through learning and art and prudence, and Dante was of this second sort. For he acquired the knowledge which he was to adorn and exemplify in his verses through attentive and laborious study of philosophy, theology, astrology, arithmetic, through the reading of history and through the turning over of many different books.

Palmieri, Bruni, Manetti: the liberation of the Florentine language aside, Dante the teacher, supreme philosopher and unrivaled example is on his way to becoming the great "Platonist"—or even more, he who has known how to attain a universal synthesis of thought. The passage in Palmieri from the prose of the *Civic Life* to the Dantesque *terza rima* of the Dantesque and neoplatonizing *City of Life* well characterizes a succession of decades under the sign of Dante—a Dante who seeks his triumphs beyond the literary field, on that of philosophy and ideology.

From 1421 many perspectives had been changing on the

very plane of thought. "O support and repose of my life," he
had been invoked by Mariotto Davanzati; and Giovanni da
Prato could attribute to him a singular credit: "The glory of
the universal language he had from Jove." However, it is not
along this line that one wishes to follow Dante's fortune—
others have already done it excellently—but along that of
ideas: not separable, certainly, from the first, but distinguish-
able. And precisely here the "civic" Dante of Bruni, already
in Palmieri interpreted with "platonic" assistance, becomes
on the one hand imitated in philosophic poems, on the other
utilized on the ground of ideology, in the new "Laurentian"
atmosphere. To tell the whole story would require a very
long discourse, which is not possible. Let some very brief
references suffice: at least a nod to the *Raccolta Aragonese*
with Poliziano's contribution [*No.* 8]; to the sonnets of
Lorenzo, which he himself commented upon in ostentatious
imitation of the *Vita Nuova* [*No.* 12]. The highest point is
reached in 1481, with Niccolò della Magna's printing of the
Commedia, offered to the Signoria with the commentary of
Cristoforo Landino [*No.* 10] and the illustrations of Sandro
Botticelli. Marsilio Ficino, in a piece of vivid rhetoric, cele-
brates the true return of Dante, that of which Dante himself
had dreamed, and his coronation in the choir of the heavens
and the gods [*No.* 9]. "Glory on high to great Apollo! Glory
to the Muses! Glory to the Graces! Peace, joy and happiness
to the Florentines, rejoicing in their now twofold sun!" As
for Landino, who had gone back to the *Convivio* for his *De
nobilitate,* here he takes the occasion to put in focus again the
whole Dante question, and the superiority of the vernacular,
and Dante's meanings and philosophic values. Nor was a
platonic transcription (especially of the *Purgatorio,* and
above all of the *Paradiso*) difficult or completely without
foundation, for one who was not afraid of some forcing and
some undue amplification. The result was a valuable thing,

even with its debts to previous commentaries. There emerged a vital and long active monument of the culture of Lorenzo's group: a singular Dante, a synthesis of concepts, which like few other works still popularized for some decades the positions of a remarkable circle of learned men.

Now, along this sunset of the century, for almost twenty-five years a history of the splendid intellectual flowering of Florence is not possible without meeting Alighieri, this Alighieri, at every step. In 1484 Pico della Mirandola feels obliged to take a position establishing a comparison between Dante, Petrarca and Lorenzo [*No. 13*]; and it is important that his detachment (especially at the beginning) from the neoplatonic movement and from the Florentine environment is expressed in a series of reservations concerning Dante, "rough, harsh and dry, and very rude and unpolished" in his style, philosophically in debt to Saint Thomas and Saint Augustine—a "social animal," certainly, but not to be exalted too much on that account, since political commitment is the first duty of the citizen: beneficial all the same, finally, if you go beneath the surface.

In contrast to Pico, Ficino had already in 1468 translated the *Monarchia* for Bernardo del Nero and Antonio di Tuccio Manetti. To it he prefixed the noted preface:

Heaven was Dante Alighieri's fatherland, Florence his place of birth. Of angelic descent, he was by profession a poetic philosopher; and although he did not talk in the Greek tongue with Plato, that sacred father of the philosophers and interpreter of the truth, he nonetheless conversed in spirit with him in such a way that he adorned his books with many platonic sayings. Through such adornments he rendered Florence so illustrious that one can just as well say "Dantean Florence" as "Florentine Dante."

According to Ficino, Dante's order is wholly platonic, constructed "drinking with Virgil's vessel from the platonic springs." And this Laurentian Dante, so platonic, is characterized to such a point that when in 1559 (after a vain Erasmian attempt) Oporinus prints the *Monarchia* for the first time at Basle, he cautions in the dedication that the treatise is not by "that celebrated old Italian poet," but by a completely different person: "a philosopher, a very acute and learned man, and once a good friend of Angelo Poliziano." It is a splitting that assumes almost an emblematic value.

Of this Dante, Mediceans and Savonarolans alike will seek the bones, or at least the recent descendants. In the name of Antonio di Tuccio Manetti, Girolamo Benivieni (Platonist, and follower of Pico and Savonarola) discourses upon the *Commedia* and the structure of the three realms, in a dialogue where there appears also one of the strangest "prophets" of the movement: Francesco da Meleto. Even Savonarola, who assails the poets, almost against his own will falls in with Dante in a way: his colleague Fra Eustachio the illuminator can recite the whole poem from memory. Benivieni, besides imitating it, will publish an edition. Between 1514 and 1515 he writes to Leo X for the bones of Dante, and recalls Bernardo Bembo's unkept promises. The Medicean Sacred Academy asks for them again; and almost too well known is the petition to the Pope in 1519, signed by Michelangelo among others, who volunteers to build the tomb of him who—with the Bible—is his book. And it would be no mere rhetorical trick to put next to the Dante who inspired Michelangelo, the Dante who served Leonardo as a philosophic-scientific source.

Whoever runs through these years again cannot but realize that Dante is not a literary fact. He is something else and much more. He is the platonic philosopher of Ficino and Landino, the prophet of the Savonarolans, the scientist of Leonardo; he is the theologian who inspires the humble Lullism of Fallamonica and the Last Judgment of Michelangelo. Strangely, in the century whose hostility to Dante is so often underlined, Dante is in reality extraordinarily present: imitated, celebrated, exalted. Even if driven back on literary ground, he is recovered on the ideological and philosophical. In the same measure in which the men of letters fight around his name, his figure becomes the symbol of a whole civilization, the object of a cult on the part of thinkers, artists, politicians. It is his greatest *"fortuna,"* which culminates and in a way concludes with Michelangelo, for whom Varchi's judgment remains valid: "I have no doubt that Michelangelo imitated Dante in his works as he did in his poetry, not only giving them that grandeur and majesty which is seen in Dante's concepts, but also striving to make, in marble or with colors, that which Dante had made in his pronouncements and with words." Michele Barbi began his still memorable study with a text of Cesare Balbo: the Cinquecento "was for Dante a century of growing and spreading glory"—of literary glory, of literary conflicts. "We," one of the most acute critics will write, "leaving to one side the sciences . . . will admire the loftiness of invention . . . the miraculously expressed emotions." Very true: and all Borghini's pages are to be reread. In the age which passes for not having understood him, from the time of Salutati to that of the Sistine Chapel, Dante had been different: an occasion of conscience and a total expression of the sense of life, not of a time but of all time: heaven and earth converging in human destiny, because we are men, and we do not leave our skin even when we declare the death of the man. And Dante, even for the most fastidious, overwhelms through having given voice to all that is human, closely bound to one time, yet beyond time—like Michelangelo.

In the course of the Cinquecento, between the judgments of Bembo [*No.* 14] and the readings of the Umidi and the Florentine Academy, between Varchi and the savage criticisms that go under the name of Rodolfo Castravilla and the answers of Jacopo Mazzoni, Dante is reduced within more actual dimensions, read and interpreted according to more precise parameters (or that propose to be such). For an age that on every hand shuns the customary definitions—which is what the Quattrocento is—for a production that cannot be well situated in the usual outlines, the Cinquecento substitutes—which is legitimate—a tranquil and proportioned vision: more deliberate historical references and more appropriate philosophical glosses, of Aristotelian philosophy. A great detachment permits a more accurate view. Great detachment, reduction—language, literature, not a total conception of things and an extraordinary and exhaustive expression, which however still seems to crop up in one of the most subtle and gifted readers of the Cinquecento: Gelli, the man of the people ("living content in my house with the bread that comes from the toil of my hands," he writes in the dedication of 1554). It had been Dante who, in a profession "so different from letters," had impelled Gelli to study Latin and philosophy and theology and all the sciences: because Dante "does not truly deserve . . . to be praised only among poets, but among all the other writers of whatever science one wishes." According to the gentle image reproduced by Gelli, in him is not so much May with its flowers, as September with its fruits. This is the great "moral," not "formal," lesson of Dante, political, philosophical, religious—the Dante in whom the great ones of the Quattrocento recognize their own ideals. The more subtle and refined literary criticism of the sixteenth century was the prelude to a profound disjunction.

I.

TRECENTO PROLOGUE

1

Coluccio Salutati

THE DEATH OF PETRARCA[1]

It may appear tactless and indecorous, great Count, to
renew for your ears what I know has just been written by
others. Nevertheless, you seem the only one of the nobility
with whom it is possible to speak about the departure of that
divine man, Petrarca. We know you cherished him with a
sincere love while he was alive; and others who boast of an
old and renowned lineage devote themselves not to literature
but to I don't know what matters. (Not to mention their
profligate activities, we see that they sweat at warfare and
hunting, and take delight in riding and fowling.) So I shall
talk with you—not with that eloquence and embellishment
which befits as great a man as you and which corresponds to
my topic, but in accord with my ability as a writer. I shall be
excused by the affection I felt for that man of distinguished
memory, and which (with your leave) I shall cherish for you.
It was not the office of so ardent a lover to pass by in complete
silence the praise of such a great man. (I believe no one in the
future will deserve such praise; or at least—and this can be
said more safely—I recall no one so far who deserved it.) I
cannot be like a tree or stone, unmoved at this neglect of

1. This letter was written about a month after Petrarca's death to Roberto
Guidi, Count of Battifolle, with whom Petrarca had begun to correspond in
1363 (see E. H. Wilkins, *Romanic Review* [1959], 3–8). It is translated from
the first volume of Salutati's *Epistolario,* ed. F. Novati (Rome, 1891).

him; for, as that reverend man Job says, my strength is not
the strength of stones, or my flesh of brass.[2] I have been
moved, I confess, at seeing extinguished not just the shining
splendor of Florence, but the light of all Italy, the light of
our age. And although he seems in his time to have yielded to
nature and laid aside the burden of our mortality, he could
nevertheless have been with us still longer and charmed us
more years with his mellifluous language. We could have
enjoyed his company; and that star of eloquence and dwell-
ing place of all the virtues, a favor granted us by the celestial
power's kindness, could have been called forth to a later
death by the same maker of all things.

When he had lived enough for nature and enough for
glory, there was no further reason for him to enjoy the light
of day and stay among mortals. There remained only to wish
and say together with the teacher of the Gentiles: "I desire to
depart and to be with Christ."[3] For what further virtue or
glory could many additional years have given him? Among
mortals, in the company of those corruptible things, what
good could be desired which he had not long since attained
by his merits and by his works, from which the dregs of all
passions had been purged? For who was more learned in
things human and divine? Who more intelligent in taking
counsel? Who more cautious in avoiding dangers? Who had a
more abundant knowledge of the past, especially what our
ancestors bequeathed to us in literary monuments? Who was
more orderly in managing or more perspicacious in foresee-
ing the outcomes of things? I shall not say how frugal his way
of life was, how sober his dress, how affable the rest of his
behavior; or how kindly and frequently he gave, and how
sparingly and rarely he would receive it back; or how he
scorned and thought little of those things in which the life of

2. Job, 6: 12.
3. Paul, Philippians, 1: 23.

mortals is entangled; or how calmly he put up with the misfortunes that exasperate our frail human condition, and how severely he scoffed at fortune's smile. He was neither broken by adversity nor softened by success. I could not easily say how great was his reverence for the heavenly powers, his respect for his elders, his equability with peers and his kindness toward inferiors. Why mention how constant was his faith, how sure his hope, how warm his charity? All these things he possessed to a more than credible or human degree. Go now, and compare him to anyone alive or dead; whom will you cite—I shall not say greater in his virtues—who is Petrarca's equal?

Moreover, what shall I say about his literary studies? Antiquity was somewhat more productive of literary men than our time, and shone forth adorned with such stars; but everyone agrees that our Petrarca flashed out so wonderfully that he seems easily to surpass any of the ancients you could oppose to him. In the liberal arts, you can see from his writings how fit his nature was. But good God, how he excelled in philosophy! This divine gift is known to be the governess of all virtues and (to borrow a word of Cicero's) [4] the expeller of vices and the mistress of all arts and sciences. I do not mean that philosophy which the modern sophists wonder at in the schools with vain, windy boastings and impudent garrulity; but rather that which refines spirits, builds virtue, washes away the filth of vice and throws light on the truth of all things without quibbling disputations. Let them rejoice in that former philosophy, those who take delight in devising "indissoluble" arguments blown together with great toil, those who are moved by the glory of scholastic training. We revere the newer philosophy and embrace it with all our mind's strength. Consider in the light of this philosophy the poems, letters and books which that man of

4. *Tusc. Disp.*, V, ii, 5.

divine genius published while alive, and you will see how proficient he was in it. As for that priestess of all sciences—philosophy's philosophy, so to speak—which probes the secrets of divinity, although it seems to exceed the limits of knowledge I would be hard put to express with what an able mind he drank of it, with what a clear intellect he absorbed it—as can be inferred from a consideration of his works.

But leaving those things aside, let us observe his eloquence, through which he clearly showed how superior he was in other human pursuits. I have reserved its praises for last, because in my judgment it is the most important. For what is greater than to rule the spirit's motions, to move your listener where you wish and then lead him back with charm and love? This, unless I am mistaken, is the strength of eloquence, this its task; the orator's whole force and power exerts itself to this end. It is of course a grand thing to embellish writing with words and maxims; but most important and most difficult, however adorned and dignified your speech, is bending the spirits of your audience. Only eloquence accomplishes all these things. Consider: since man was begotten for the sake of man, God put reason in command of each man's appetite, to guide and regulate, from the mind's summit, the turbulent movements of the spirit; and in addition he bestowed upon him eloquence (which man has in common with no other living creature), so that if his neighbor's reason has been put to sleep by corrupt behavior or the gross body's burden, he will have means to rouse him with the fires of mutual affection. A neighbor's eloquence can build where nature has failed and restore what bad habits have usurped. Since this is the case, who could deny that man's greatest glory consists in richly ornamented speech? Therefore, although the extent of Petrarca's capability in this respect is obvious, I shall digress to praise him more fully. Please do not shudder at the length of my letter.

Although what we call the faculty of speaking eloquently is the same everywhere you are engaged, it is nevertheless carried on in a twofold way: melody either rushes forth abundantly with free rein, in prose, or is compressed by continuous metrical constraints. The former, which proceeds more freely, is divided into formal speech and conversation; so that it is used either in debates or in quiet discussion, between which there is such a difference that (according to Cicero's testimony) [5] among the Greeks, whose glory was great in all literary pursuits, only Demetrius of Phalerum seems to have gained renown in both. (Nevertheless, though charming he is affirmed to have been a not very powerful speaker.) Petrarca's thousands of letters, in which he used each style as the occasion warranted, show what grandeur and ornament and strength he had in these divisions of eloquence. The same is shown by his many books: for example, the *Invectives Against a Doctor,* which anyone regarding them attentively will agree (*pace* Cicero) easily surpass the *Verrines* and the *Philippics* and the *Catilinarian Orations* themselves; and *The Life of Solitude* and his sacred work, *Remedies for Good and Evil Fortune;* and the book *On His Own Ignorance and That of Many Others;* the book of *Fragments*[6]—all of which he finished and published—and his *Lives of Famous Men,* which I know was composed by him, though I am uncertain whether he published it. O, magnanimous Count, if we should be permitted to gather all these books together and nourish ourselves with reading them, believe me, if anyone maintains that Cicero was his equal in oratorical strength, he would doubtless say that our Petrarca surpassed that father of Roman eloquence in verbal adorn-

5. *De Off.,* I, i, 3.
6. This is how Petrarca referred to his *Canzoniere.* Apparently Salutati assumed that a *Libellus fragmentorum* would be a Latin work; see B. L. Ullman, *Studies in the Italian Renaissance* (Rome, 1955) , pp. 213–214.

ment and gravity of thought, whether he makes the forum
resound or speaks and writes in his room.

Moreover in that other form of eloquence, which goes forward with measured feet, compressed in verse, Petrarca's
divine *Bucolics* inform us of his ability; the fame of his *Africa*
proves it; and many other verses published by him confirm it.
I should like to add one point, that very few of the ancients,
whose works we admire and cherish, excelled at both prose
and poetry. Cicero himself, the fount of eloquence, was an
admirable prose writer but a failure in verse. (Read his book
On Divination and see how many verses he quotes from his
translations of Aratus. Were they not bolstered by Cicero's
authority, I believe you would deny them any success at
all.) [7] On the other hand we read that Virgil pleaded one case
before the judges, with a very unhappy outcome; was scared
away from oratory; and turned to poetry.[8] In this he surpassed all the Greeks and Latins; but it is still strange that
none of so great a man's prose is extant. Believe me, though,
he was as inferior in prose as he was superior in poetry.[9]
Therefore we may proudly and not unjustly prefer our
Francesco to each of them, since he was so gloriously successful in both prose and verse.[10]

Finally, when Quintilian set Latin against Greek literature, Cicero was matched with Demosthenes, the most powerful Greek orator; and Virgil alone was set against Homer,
Hesiod and Theocritus, who were renowned in poetry among
the Greeks.[11] (Great praise for that bard of ours, to have

7. Salutati must rather have had in mind the *De Natura Deorum,* in which
are inserted numerous verses from the *Phaenomena.*

8. Donatus, *Vita P. Verg. Mar.,* VI.

9. Seneca, *Controv.,* III, 8.

10. Cf. Petrarca, *Sen.,* XVII, 2 (to Boccaccio): "You counsel me to be
contented—I quote you literally—with having perhaps equaled Virgil in
verse (as you assert) and Cicero in prose" (trans. Robinson and Rolfe, reprinted in *Petrarch,* David Thompson, ed. [New York, 1971], p. 239).

11. Quintilian, *Inst. Orat.,* X, i.

been compared with the three princes of poetry.) And
though insolent Greece set itself before or equal to Latium in
other respects, it admitted that Seneca surpassed any Greek
moral writer. But we have someone we can prefer (not just
compare) to antiquity and to Greece itself: this Francesco
Petrarca, whose name no oblivion will ever efface, and whom
nature seems to have brought forth so that even though eloquence had thus far yielded herself completely to no one,[12]
there would be at last one man in whom she showed her full
force. In poetry we may set our Petrarca against that divine
Virgil and the Greek bards whom he rivaled and surpassed,
while in prose we may set him before Cicero and Demosthenes, and in moral writing before Seneca himself. I say
nothing of compositions in his mother tongue, written in
eight and six verses, or fewer, whose rhymes tickle the ears of
the common people. Everyone agrees that he excelled his
follow countryman Dante Alighieri (himself a truly divine
man) and all the others.

Farewell then, great man! You have won eternal fame with
your virtues, the splendor of your wisdom and the light of
your eloquence: all antiquity cannot equal you. Our age,
illumined by the brightness of your name, will (unless I
deceive myself) go down in history as worthy of admiration;
you have acquired the immortality of fame not only for yourself, but also for our times! But why try to enclose the praises
of this famous man within the narrow confines of a letter,
when innumerable volumes would not hold them? Better to
have passed over the praises of so great a man in silence than
to have said too little!

But let me return to where I began. Should I not, then,
grieve that so great a sun has set for us? Let all our age weep;
let Latium and Florence itself overflow with tears; let rhet-

---

12. Seneca, *Controv.*, III, 17.

oric and the Muses weep; let the whole trivium and quadrivium weep; let bereaved poetry weep and history go into
mourning; and finally, whatever outstanding thing is entrusted to literature, and all who delight in these pursuits, let
them weep, lament and grieve. And you, and I, and others,
whom he kindly thought worthy of his friendship, let us
mourn for him. Alas, how little man knows of fate (as our
Virgil says).[13] I had just about finished revising verses in
which I urged him to publish the *Africa,* and I was going to
send them to him as soon as a messenger had made himself
available. But behold: a dismal report has been the messenger of so lamentable a death. Thus my poem has remained
unfinished, much the way he probably abandoned his *Africa.*
Alas, unpropitious month of July, in which the heavenly
power determined that such a light be extinguished from the
world. Were it permitted, I'd drag you out of the calendar
and relegate you to perpetual mourning among the unlucky
days marking disasters such as Cannae. Alas! Whose advice
shall we ask about the riddles of poetry? Whom shall we
question about arcane matters? Whom shall we approach
concerning the rules of rhetoric? Who will instill moral
precepts into our ears? Who will clear up authors' obscure
sayings? Who will harmonize differing historical accounts?
Whom shall we hear writing more frankly, or singing in
verse? Alas, was unjust, blind fortune able to seize him from
us? Was death not ashamed to thrust that noble spirit from its
corporeal abode? But these are words to the wind: implacable
fate and the cruel hand of death have removed him from us
utterly.

But what have you accomplished, death? When we come
into your power we shall get him back even against your
wishes, since the better part of him is alive. That divine gift

13. *Aeneid,* X, 501.

partaking of reason lives on; you have been cruel only to the body which it vivified. Over neither have you any further sway, for his body has returned to its resting place and his soul to its creator. Even while alive, O death, he had his victory over you, he overcame you, he triumphed over you. He procured himself the other immortality, over which you have no power: fame, and eternal renown. Present and future ages will sing his praises and he will be celebrated by the threefold realm of shades. For you there is left a foul, vile victory over his body alone. Do not boast, O death: since the best part of him lives on, he has escaped your violent force. Lead in triumph those whom you have to tear away from the seductive fellowship of these perishable things, not those who come willingly.

But why have I carried on in such a troubled and angry fashion? As a mortal I weep the death of mortals—what could be more foolish and unjust? I grieve at a friend's glorious reward—what could be more spiteful? For although I feel tormented by an inestimable loss, I should have balanced my misfortune with his good fortune. And so let us wipe away our tears and find comfort now in our Francesco, since God and nature have done well—no, excellently—by him. In departing, he has freed himself from whatever was burdening his mind's keenness and his spirit's vigor. Summoned from heaven to his stars, he now contemplates his creator face to face, than which nothing is more delightful. As much as immortal things differ from mortal, and divine celestial things excel what is human and earthly, to this degree has his eloquence increased; and he composes hymns of praise to the creator of all things; and mingling with the happy spirits he wonders at and makes glad those eternal gyres; and now at last he understands that what we think of as life is really the death of the soul. Furthermore, every offense against God's majesty committed through the contagion of mortal things;

every good vow of which the human condition becomes
incapable; every cloud of ignorance darkening the purity of
our intellect; every slippery fall from virtue's summit that
has been prepared for us—he beholds them now through
immortal eyes with true knowledge, and I know that while
he was alive, and when he suffered at the point of death, he
urged this to himself with sound reasons. For if Hermes
Trismegistus, a pagan, discussed this same thing at the very
end of his life, what ought we to think about our Petrarca,
who was not only steeped in philosophy but also enlightened
by the doctrine and admonitions of the Christian faith?
Hermes, when the nearness of death was pressing upon him,
is said to have spoken this way to a circle of friends who were
standing by:

Thus far, dear friends, I have remained among you in banishment, a pilgrim and an exile; but now, completely restored to a
sound condition, I am called back to my fatherland, where all
who have deserved to inhabit it are rendered free from death and
corruption. I already seem to be filled with a wonderful sweetness,
thinking that I shall be joined to the creator and, having escaped
completely our mutable condition, share in inviolable and perfect goodness. And so do not mourn me as if I were dead, when
the better part of me has left this body behind and I seem to
have flown from the land of the living. Now here together with
you I am dead; but then, when I have been at last restored to life,
I shall await you in the presence of the great maker of all things.[14]

A pagan could say this, with reason his only guide; and
with all due respect to him and to Greece, he cannot be
placed on a par with our Petrarca, even if antiquity did
devote divine honors to him in admiration for his virtue.
Should we not believe that Petrarca, the most Christian of

14. Drawn from a treatise in dialogue form entitled *De Consolatione
Fraterna*.

men, spoke with far more distinction and convinced himself with more certainty than Hermes?

To conclude my letter at last (so that I won't, as Jerome says to Rufinus, seem to have written an *Orestes*),[15] let us rejoice in him and his felicity; let us be glad that he has finally been freed from the prison of his body and seen the end of his life while we are still alive. For now we can say with assurance that he has done that most difficult of all things, preserved the glory of his fame for the whole length of his life. And you, Francesco, let us render you your due and wish you well with an ancient (if pagan) word: *Vale*. When nature summons, we shall follow you in like manner.

I had this to write in praise of our Petrarca—little, to be sure, in comparison with the subject, but long enough for the measure of my knowledge, and too much considering how busy I am. I wished, illustrious Count, to place before your eyes the life, character and fame of that man, whose memory may—although you do strive after virtue with a swift course— dispose you to push forward with your purpose. And keep in mind that those who cling with all their spirit to perishable things, and are dead in their body, have perished after leaving it unless God's mercy looks after them.

Farewell.

Florence, August 16, 1374

---

15. Jerome drew the phrase from Juvenal, *Sat.*, I, 6.

2

IN QUEST OF DANTE[1]

Distinguished man, excellent brother, dear friend, I am anxious to have a correct copy of our Dante's divine work. Believe me, no poem so far is loftier in style or more elegant in invention or of greater weight, when you consider the subject, the diction or the treatment. Where do we have more fully and clearly a reasoned differentiation of the three-fold style? Where will you find so many great things joined more finely and beautifully? Where could you find more important matters set forth in more fitting words? In short, dear Niccolò, we can point out nothing loftier, nothing more embellished, nothing more polished and nothing more profound in knowledge than those three cantiche. Things that are single and separate in others have been comprehended by him fully and simultaneously. There moral, philosophical and theological precepts shine in wondrous fashion; there rhetorical figures of thought and language are evident in such splendor that you would be hard put to find such great embellishment elsewhere, even in the greatest authors. There the laws and ways and tongues of all ages and peoples, and a wonderful historical compendium, blaze like stars in the firmament, with so great majesty that no one as yet has been able to surpass or equal him in that style.

1. This letter was written, probably in 1399, to Niccolò da Tuderano, Chancellor of Ravenna for Guido da Polenta and his successors. It is translated from the third volume of Salutati's *Epistolario*, ed. F. Novati (Rome, 1896).

What is the point of all this? So that you will wonder less at seeing me long so passionately to find a correct text. I cannot say how annoyed I am at that corruption which has attacked all books. Of the books of Petrarca and Boccaccio, hardly a codex is now found faithfully written and not departing greatly from the original. They are in fact not copies but imitations of copies. True copies are images of the originals; but what we have for copies are so different from the originals that they fall short of them more than statues do of the men whose likenesses they are. Statues, although they have mouths, say nothing, but our copies do something worse: they often speak contrary to their originals. And although it is a universal misfortune, in this book it has crept in more extensively since ignorant common men cannot copy skillfully an original by a learned man.

But now I have heard that Menghino Mezzani, cardinal or canon of the church of Ravenna, and formerly a close friend of our Dante, was a very learned student of this book and wrote about it with care. I hear—and I think it is true—that his books have come into the hands of those great lords of mine; wherefore I should like to ask you, by heaven and hell and whatever dear and honorable is found in friendship, to help me see and have that man's Dante and what he wrote on him. I hope that I found so much favor in their eyes that they will in no wise object to pleasing me concerning this.

Farewell, and if you love me be mindful of me and of this matter.

Florence, October 2

II.

CLASSICISM AND
CIVIC HUMANISM

3

LEONARDO BRUNI

DIALOGUES

To Pier Paulo Vergerio[1]

INTRODUCTION

There is a wise old saying that to be happy one must first of all have an illustrious and renowned native land. In this respect I am unhappy, Pietro, because my land[2] has been overthrown and reduced almost to nothing by repeated blows of fortune; but I do enjoy the solace of living in this city,[3] which seems by far to surpass and excel all others. It is eminent for its numerous inhabitants, its splendid buildings and its great undertakings; and, in addition, some seeds of the liberal arts and of all human culture, which once seemed completely dead, remained here and grow day by day and very soon, I believe, will bring forth no inconsiderable light. If only you could have dwelt together with me in this city! I

---

1. A pupil of Salutati's, who had returned to Padua in the spring of 1400. The Introduction and the First Dialogue date from 1401, while the Second Dialogue, which cites Bruni's *Laudatio* (of post-1402 origin) must represent a later phase of his thought; see now Hans Baron, "Chronology and Historical Certainty: The Dates of Bruni's *Laudatio and Dialogi*," in *From Petrarch to Leonardo Bruni* (Chicago and London, 1968), pp. 102–137. On Vergerio's own life of Petrarca, see Baron, *The Crisis of the Early Italian Renaissance* (rev. 1-vol. ed.), pp. 263–264. The *Dialogi* are translated from *Prosatori Latini del Quattrocento*, ed. E. Garin (Milan and Naples, 1952).

2. Arezzo; hence Bruni was called Aretinus (Aretino).

3. I.e., Florence, where Bruni had settled and was later to become chancellor.

have no doubt that your companionship would have made my studies lighter in the past and more pleasant for the future. However, fortune or your own affairs determined that you be separated from me against your will and mine, and I cannot help longing for you. Nevertheless, every day I eagerly enjoy what I have left of you, for although mountains and valleys in between separate your body from me, neither distance nor forgetfulness will ever part you from my affectionate memory. Hardly a day goes by without my often recalling you to mind.

But although I always long for your presence, I especially miss you when we are discussing any of those topics you delighted in while you were here; as recently, when there was a disputation at Coluccio's house, I can't say how much we wished you were present. You certainly would have been impressed by the worthiness of the topic being debated, and by the worthiness of the participants; for you know that hardly anyone has greater authority than Coluccio, and Niccolò,[4] who was opposing him, is a ready speaker and a very spirited challenger. I have described that disputation in this book I am sending you, so that even though you are absent you may enjoy our advantages to some extent. Most of all, I have tried to preserve each one's manner accurately— with what success, it will be up to you to judge.

BOOK I

Since the feast days for Christ's Resurrection were being celebrated and my good friend Niccolò and I had come together, we decided to go visit Coluccio Salutati, easily the

4. On Niccoli (1364–1437), see Vespasiano, *Renaissance Princes, Popes and Prelates* (New York, 1963), pp. 395–402. Baron has been rather harsh on Niccoli; a more sympathetic discussion is offered by Ernst Gombrich, "From the Revival of Letters to the Reform of the Arts: Niccolò Niccoli and Filippo Brunelleschi," in *Essays in the History of Art Presented to Rudolph Wittkower,* ed. Douglas Fraser, et al. (London, 1967), pp. 71–82.

leading man of this age in wisdom and eloquence and integrity. We had not gone far when we were met by Roberto Rossi,[5] a friend of ours and a man devoted to studying the liberal arts. He asked where we were going; and when he heard what we had in mind he thought it was a good idea and followed along. On our arrival, Coluccio greeted us in a pleasant, friendly way and bade us take a seat; we sat down and exchanged the small talk which is usual when friends first get together; then silence ensued. We were waiting for Coluccio to initiate the conversation; and he thought that we had come to him with some purpose in mind or to propose a topic for discussion. But as the silence dragged on, and it was clear that his visitors had made no beginning, Coluccio turned to us with that expression he assumes when he is about to speak carefully; and when he saw he had our attention, he began a discussion of this sort.

"Words cannot express, young men, how delighted I am with your presence: whether because of your character, or the studies we have in common, or the respect you pay me, I regard you with extraordinary friendship and affection. But I disapprove of you in one matter, and that a very important one. In other things which pertain to your studies I perceive in you the care and vigilance necessary for men who wish to be called discreet and attentive. But in this one respect I see that you are dull and have insufficient regard for your own advantage: you neglect to make a habit of practicing disputation. I do not know if you would find anything more advantageous for your studies. In the name of the gods, for examining and discussing subtle matters what could be more efficacious than disputation, where the topic is placed as it were stage center and observed by many eyes, so that there is nothing in it which can escape or deceive the view of all?

5. Rossi was Cosimo de' Medici's teacher; see Vespasiano, *op. cit.* (p. 213) for a brief but charming portrait.

When the soul is weary and weakened and shrinks from these studies, what could renew and refresh it more than discussions carried on in a gathering, where you are strongly fired to read and learn thoroughly—by glory, if you have overcome others, or by shame if you have been overcome. What sharpens the intellect, rendering it more clever and versatile, better than disputation, since in a brief space of time one must apply one's self to the topic and thence reflect, discourse, make inferences and conclusions? So that it is easy to understand how a mind stimulated by this practice becomes swifter at discussing other things. There is no need to say how it polishes our speech, how it brings it under our ready command. You yourselves can see this in the case of many who read a lot of books and profess themselves men of letters, but cannot speak Latin except with their books because they have refrained from this practice.

"And so, since I am eager for your advantage and wish to see you as distinguished as possible in your studies, I am rightly somewhat angry with you for neglecting this habit of disputation, from which flow so many benefits. It is absurd to talk to yourself and deliberate upon many things when you are all alone and surrounded by walls, and then grow dumb, as if you knew nothing, when in a gathering before men's eyes. And it is absurd to pursue with great labor things possessing some one advantage, but be unwilling to engage in disputation, from which arise a great many advantages—and very pleasantly, at that. We should not approve a farmer who could cultivate his whole estate and instead just plowed some barren woodlands, leaving the richest part uncultivated. In the same way we ought to blame a man who could perform all the employments called for by his studies but instead devotes great care to the others, however important, while disdaining the practice of disputation, from which so many rich fruits are gathered.

"I recollect that when I was still a young student of grammar in Bologna I spent every hour of every day in disputation. I challenged my comrades and questioned my teachers. And this was not something I did in boyhood but then abandoned as I grew older. Throughout my life nothing was more pleasing to me, and I sought nothing so much, as getting together with learned men whenever possible and explaining to them what I was deliberating upon and undecided about, and asking for their judgment.

"I know that you all (especially you, Niccolò, since you were very friendly with him and were always at his house) remember the theologian Luigi Marsili,[6] a man of penetrating genius and remarkable eloquence, who died seven years ago. While he was still alive I often visited him for the purpose I just mentioned. And if sometimes, as often happens, I had not prepared at home a subject on which I wished to speak with him, I did my preparation en route. As you know, he lived across the Arno, and I had made the river a sort of mark, so that from the time I crossed it until I reached his house I occupied myself with the topics I proposed to talk about with him. After arriving I used to draw out the conversation for hours; and yet I was always unwilling to leave, for my soul could never have enough of that man's presence. Immortal gods, what force and copiousness of expression he had! What a memory! For he had a mastery not only of what pertains to religion, but also those things which we call Gentile. He was always talking of Cicero, Virgil, Seneca and the other ancients: he often cited not only their opinions and sayings, but also their very words, in such a way that they seemed not drawn from another but rather his own productions. I was never able to bring forward anything that seemed new to him; he had long since beheld and known it

6. An Augustinian monk at the Convent of S. Spirito. He died in 1394.

all. But I heard many things from him, I learned much from him, and by the authority of that man I confirmed many things about which I was in doubt.

" 'But what's the point of talking so much about yourself?' someone will say. 'Are you the only disputant?' By no means. I could have named a great many who frequently did the same thing, but I preferred to speak about myself, so that on the basis of my own knowledge I could corroborate for you what great usefulness there is in disputation; for I, who have lived to this day in such a fashion that I have spent all my time and effort in the endeavor to learn, feel I have obtained such great fruits from these discussions or conversations which I call disputations, that I ascribe to this one thing a great part of what I have learned. For this reason I beseech you, young men, to add to your praiseworthy and splendid labors this one practice which thus far has escaped you, so that furnished with its manifold benefits you may the more easily attain your goal."

Then Niccolò said: "You are perfectly right, Salutati. I believe nothing could easily be found which would confer more on our studies than disputation. Nor are you the first to tell me this: I often heard Luigi himself—your mention of whom almost brought me to tears—saying the same thing. And that Chrysoloras, from whom they[7] learned Greek, once when I was present (which, as you know, I often was) particularly exhorted his pupils to talk over some topic among themselves. But his exhortation was simple and bare, as if the usefulness of this were evident; he did not point out its force and power. You, on the other hand, have so presented it with your words, have so revealed its every effect, that you have placed its value clearly before our eyes. And so I cannot say how pleasing your discourse has been to me.

7. I.e., Bruni and Rossi. Chrysoloras, who taught Greek in Florence from 1397 to 1400, also had among his noted pupils Palla Strozzi, Guarino, Francesco Barbaro and Pier Paulo Vergerio (Vespasiano, *op. cit.*, p. 235).

"Nevertheless, Coluccio, if in this matter we have not employed ourselves the way you think necessary, the fault is not ours but the times'; wherefore, I beseech you, see that you do not wrongfully become angry with us your friends. If you will in any way show that we could well have done it, for our neglect of it we will equally bear not only words from you, but also lashes. However, if we have been born in a time when so great a disturbance of all learning, so great a loss of books has occurred that no one could talk about the least thing without great impudence, you will certainly excuse us if we have preferred to seem silent rather than impudent. I do not think you are one to be pleased by empty chattering; nor are you urging us to do so, but rather to speak so authoritatively, so consistently, that we appear to know and feel what we are saying. And so one must have a proper grasp of the topic he wishes to discuss; and not just that, but a knowledge of the consequences, antecedents, causes, effects— in short, of everything pertaining to the topic. Without such knowledge no disputant can but appear absurd. You see what a mass of things this entails, for everything is wonderfully connected and one cannot know a few things well without knowing many things well.

"But enough of this and back to the point. For my part, Coluccio, in this wretched age and amidst such a dearth of books, I do not see what power of disputation anyone could achieve. At this time what art, what learning can be found which has not been displaced or completely corrupted? Place before your eyes whichever of them you wish, and consider what it is now and what it was formerly; then you will understand that they have all been reduced to the point where one must utterly despair.

"Take philosophy, to consider especially the mother of all the other liberal arts and from whose fountains is derived all this human culture of ours. Philosophy was once brought from Greece into Italy by Cicero and watered by that golden stream of eloquence. In his books the principle of every philosophy was expounded and the individual schools of the philosophers set forth. This, it seems to me, was very effective in rousing men's studies; for whoever approached philosophy set directly before himself the authorities to follow, and he learned not only to defend his own positions but also to refute those of others. Hence there were Stoics, Academics, Peripatetics, Epicureans; hence were born all the contentions and dissensions among them. If only those books still existed and our forefathers had not been so slothful! They preserved for us Cassiodorus and Alcidus and other nonsense of this sort,[8] which men of even moderate learning have never cared to read; but the books of Cicero, than which the Muses of the Latin language never produced anything fairer, they suffered to perish from neglect. This could only have been the result of the greatest ignorance, for if they had attained even a superficial acquaintance with them they certainly would never have neglected Cicero's works, which were endowed with such eloquence that they would easily avoid being scorned by a not uncultivated reader. But since a great part of those books has perished, and the remaining ones are so faulty that they are not far from death, how do you think we are to learn philosophy at this time?

"But there are many masters of this knowledge who promise to teach it. O splendid philosophers of our time, who teach what they do not know! I cannot wonder sufficiently at them, how they learned philosophy while being ignorant of letters; for when they speak they utter more solecisms than words. And so I should rather hear them snoring than speaking. But if anyone should ask them on whose authority and precepts they rely in this splendid wisdom of theirs, they say: the Philosopher's, by which they mean Aristotle's. And

8. Alcidus is the presumed author of a consolatory dialogue (probably medieval) often cited by Salutati.

when there is need to confirm something or other, they bring
forth the sayings in these books which they claim to be
Aristotle's—words harsh, awkward, dissonant, which would
wear out anyone's ears. The Philosopher says this, they tell
us. It is impious to contradict him, and for them *ipse dixit*
has the force of truth, as if he had been the only philosopher,
or his sayings were as fixed as those which Pythian Apollo
gave forth from his holy sanctuary.

"Not that I say this to censure Aristotle; I have no war
with that very wise man, only with the folly of these Aristo-
telians. If they were simply ignorant, they would be, if not
praiseworthy, at least to be tolerated in these wretched times.
But now, when so much arrogance has been joined to their
ignorance that they call and esteem themselves wise, who
could bear them with equanimity? This is what I feel about
them, Coluccio: not even in the least thing do I believe they
rightly grasp what Aristotle thought. And I have a most
authoritative witness to this, whom I shall bring before you.
Who? The very father of the Latin language, Marcus Tullius
Cicero—whose three names I quote this way, Salutati, so that
he will be longer in my mouth. He is that pleasant for me."

"You're right, Niccolò," said Coluccio, "for no one is more
to be loved and delighted in than our Cicero. But where does
he say that? I do not know the passage."

"This was written by Cicero at the beginning of the
Topica; for when the lawyer Trebatius had proposed to a
certain great rhetorician that he explain to him the meaning
of those topics expounded by Aristotle, and the rhetorician
had replied that he 'didn't know those Aristotelian teach-
ings,' Cicero wrote that he 'was not at all surprised at the
rhetorician's not knowing that philosopher, who is unknown
to the philosophers themselves, except for a very few.'[9] Does

9. *Topica,* I, 2–3.

it not seem to you that Cicero keeps this slothful herd from the fold? Does it not seem that he opposes those who impudently enrol themselves in Aristotle's family? 'Except for a very few,' he says. Will they dare to say they are among those very few? Yes, they are impudent enough to do so; but let them not deceive us. At the time Cicero said this it was more difficult to find unlearned men than it now is to find learned ones (for we know that the Latin language never flourished more than in Cicero's time) ; and nevertheless he speaks the way we have just explained. The philosophers themselves, then, except for a very few, were unacquainted with Aristotle at the time when every art and learning flourished, when there was a great number of learned men, when everyone was no less learned in Greek than in Latin letters and savored him in the original. If, when all that was the case, the philosophers themselves—except for a very few—were still ignorant of Aristotle, in this great shipwreck of learning, amidst our great dearth of learned men, will those who know nothing— to whom not only Greek, but indeed even Latin letters are unknown—will they not be ignorant of Aristotle? Believe me, Coluccio, it is impossible for them to grasp anything rightly, especially since those books which they say are Aristotle's have suffered such a great transformation that were anyone to bring them to Aristotle himself, he would not recognize them as his own any more than his own dogs recognized Actæon (who had been turned into a stag). For Cicero says that Aristotle was devoted to eloquence and wrote with an incredible pleasantness. But now we see these books of Aristotle's— if they are even to be considered his—troublesome and harsh to read and entangled in such obscurity that no one except the Sibyl or Oedipus would understand them. Wherefore let those splendid philosophers stop avowing this wisdom of theirs. They are not bright enough to attain it if there were the possibility of learning; and even if they were extremely intelligent, I see no such possibility at this time. But enough concerning Aristotle.

"What about dialectic, an art very necessary for disputation? Does it possess a flourishing realm, and has it endured no calamity in this war of ignorance? Not at all, for it has been assaulted even by that barbarism which dwells across the ocean. What peoples! I shudder even at their names: Ferabrich, Buser, Occam, and others of this sort, all of whom seem to have drawn their names from the throng of Rhadamanthus. And what is there, Coluccio—to leave off this joking—what is there in dialectic which has not been confounded by British sophisms? What that has not been separated from that old, true way of disputation and brought to absurdity and frivolity?

"I can say the same about grammar, about rhetoric, and about almost all the other arts; but I do not wish to be verbose in proving the obvious. To what cause shall we attribute it, Coluccio, that for so many years now no one has been found who had any distinction in these things? Men do not lack ability, or the will to learn; but in my opinion this disturbance of knowledge and lack of books has so closed off all the ways to learning that even should there be someone endowed with great ability and desire to learn, he would be impeded by such difficult circumstances that he could not achieve what he wished. For no one without instruction, without teachers, without books can attain any excellence in his studies. Since we have been deprived of the possibility of such things, who then will wonder if no one for a long time now has come near that greatness of the ancients? For a while now, though, Salutati, I have been talking with something of a red face, for you by your presence seem to refute and overthrow my speech. You are certainly the one who in wisdom and eloquence has surpassed—or surely equaled—those ancients whom we customarily admire so much. But I'll tell you what I feel about you—and not, by Hercules, for the sake of flattery. It seems to me that by your extraordinary and almost divine ability you have been able to achieve this, even lacking those things without which others are unable to do so; and so you alone must be excepted from my discussion. Let us talk about others, products of an ordinary nature. If they are not particularly learned, who will be so hard a judge as to blame them rather than ascribing it to the fault of the times and this general disorder? Do we not see what an ample and beautiful patrimony these times of ours have been deprived of? Where are the books of Marcus Varro—almost by themselves they could have made men learned—in which there was an exposition of the Latin language, a knowledge of things human and divine, and every sort of wisdom and learning? Where are the histories of Livy, of Sallust, of Pliny, or innumerable others? Where are the numerous volumes of Cicero? O wretched and miserable condition of these times! It would certainly take me all day to name those of whom our age has been deprived.

"And in such straits you, Coluccio, say you become angry with us because we do not keep our tongues flapping in disputation. Do we not hear that Pythagoras, who among all peoples has a great name for wisdom, used to give his disciples this precept especially: that they should maintain a five years' silence? And rightly, for that very wise man considered nothing less suitable than for men to dispute about things they do not grasp properly. And those whose master was Pythagoras, the most eminent of philosophers, used to do this not without praise; shall we—deprived as we are of masters, teachers, books—not be able to do this without reproof? It is not fair, Coluccio; therefore be just with us in this matter as you are wont to be in others, and lay aside this irritation of yours. We have given you no cause for anger."

When Niccolò had spoken and been heard by everyone

with great attention, a brief silence ensued. Then, looking at him, Salutati said: "Niccolò, you have never been so forceful in opposition, so authoritative in discoursing! For as our poet says, you were something more than I supposed. Although I have always considered you uniquely cut out for these studies, I still never thought there was in you such capability as you have now shown in speaking. And so, if you please, let us leave off this whole disputation about disputation."

At this point Roberto said: "Proceed, Salutati, for it is not becoming that you, who have just now urged disputation upon us, should abandon the present disputation." "For my part," replied Coluccio, "I now begin to fear I have roused a sleeping lion, as they say. But I should like to know from you, Roberto, whether you agree with me or with Niccolò. I have no doubts about Leonardo: I see his every opinion so accords with Niccolò's that I think he would rather be wrong with him than right with me."

Then I said: "Salutati, I have an equally high regard for you and Niccolò; so consider me a fair judge, although I am aware that my cause no less than Niccolò's is being pleaded in this discussion." "But I," said Roberto, "shall not reveal what I think until each of you has argued his case through. So proceed, as you have begun."

"I shall proceed," said Coluccio, "and easily refute him. For this is what I think: that elaborate speech which he used a while ago serves not so much to justify as to condemn him. How so? Because what he was attempting to prove with his words was in truth being refuted by his speech. Why? Because in justifying himself he bewailed the decadence of the times and said that all capability of disputation had been taken away; but he himself in proving this disputed very finely. What then? Does this condemn him? I think so. On what account? Because this argument cannot stand: it is contradictory to deny that something can happen and then forthwith do it—unless perhaps he is endowed with some surpassing acuteness of ability, so that he can of course do what others cannot. If I grant him this I shall free myself from the great debt with which he burdened me a while back, by setting me above even those ancients whom we are accustomed to admire. But I will not grant you this, Niccolò, nor will I arrogate so much to myself; and I am confident that there are a great many who in keenness of ability could excel me and equal you."

Here Roberto said: "Before you go any further, Coluccio, let me interrupt you for a moment. As I see it, you must be contradicting yourself; for if Niccolò—whom we know has given infrequent attention to disputation—was eloquent enough in responding (which you seem to admit), why are you so angry with us for not engaging frequently in disputations, since one can do all right in his studies without it?"

Coluccio replied: "Because I considered it very useful, I urged you to dispute; for I wish to see you distinguished in every aspect of culture. I admit that I was pleased by Niccolò's speech; and he lacked neither elegance nor subtlety. But if he was so forceful in responding without the practice of disputation, which could especially effect this, what do you suppose he would have done if he had given attention to this matter?"

Since Roberto was silent and showed assent by his expression, Coluccio turned to Niccolò and said: "It is right for you, Niccolò, to grant what Roberto does; for great is the force of practice, great its effects. There is almost nothing so harsh, nothing so rough, that constant use will not soften and polish. Do you not see how the orators, almost all with one voice, declare that art without practice is of little avail? What about in military matters, in competitions, in short, in everything? Has anything been found to be as effective as practice?

We then, if we are wise, will believe that practice has the same efficacy in our studies, and we will bestow care upon it and not neglect it. The practice of our studies moreover is conversation, inquiry, and the pursuit of those things that are deliberated in our studies—in a word, disputation. If you think we have at this time been deprived of the capability of these things, on account of this—as you say—disturbance, you are greatly in error. That the liberal arts have suffered something of a fall I shall never deny; nevertheless they have not been so extinguished that those who devote themselves to them cannot become learned and wise. Nor, even when these arts flourished, did it please everyone to reach the summit. There were more, like Neoptolemus,[10] who were satisfied with a little than there were who wished to apply themselves altogether to philosophy; and nothing prevents our doing the same today. Finally, Niccolò, you must take care lest while you wish only for the impossible you scorn and disregard even what is possible. All Cicero's books are not extant? But some remain, and no small part at that. I wish we grasped them rightly, for we should not have such fear of being called ignorant. Varro is lost? That is deplorable, I admit, and hard to bear; but still there are Seneca's books and many others, which could fill Varro's place if we were not so fastidious. And would that we knew as much—or even wished to learn as much—as these books which are now extant can teach us. But as I have just said, we are too fastidious: we desire what is lacking and disdain what we have. We should on the contrary use whatever is at hand and banish from our minds the desire for what is not, since thinking about it does us no good.

"Wherefore see to it, I beg you, that you do not transfer your fault elsewhere and wish to impute to the times what must be imputed to yourself—although I am in no way led to

10. Cf. Cicero, *Tusc. Disp.,* II, 1.

think, Niccolò, that you have not attained everything that can be learned at this time, for I know your diligence, attentiveness and acuteness. Accordingly, I should like you to think that what I said just now was spoken more to oppose your words than to attack you.

"But I wish to leave off these things; they are too obvious to be the subject of a disputation. However, I cannot think what led you to say that for a long time now there has been no one who had any excellence in these studies; for to pass over the others, can you consider not outstanding at least three men whom our city has borne in these times, Dante, Francesco Petrarca and Giovanni Boccaccio, who by the consensus of all are exalted to the heavens? For my part I do not see—and by Hercules, I am not influenced by their being my fellow citizens—why they should not be numbered among the ancients in every aspect of human culture. In fact, if Dante had employed another style of writing, I should not be content to compare him with our ancients but should even place him before the Greeks themselves. And so, Niccolò, if you knowingly passed them by, you must tell us your reason for disdaining them; but if they escaped you through some forgetfulness, you displease me for not having fixed in your memory the men who are your city's praise and glory."

Niccolò retorted: "What Dantes are you reminding me of? What Petrarcas? What Boccaccios? Do you think I judge according to the opinions of the populace, so that I approve or disapprove what the multitude does? Not at all, for when I praise something, I constantly wish my reason for doing so to be clear to me. But I have always been suspicious of the multitude, and not without cause, for its judgments are so corrupted that they bring me more ambiguity than firmness. And so do not be surprised if concerning this (so to speak) triumvirate of yours you observe that my opinion differs considerably from the people's. What is there in them which should seem admirable or praiseworthy to any one? For to begin with Dante, to whom you do not prefer even Virgil himself, do we not often see him erring in such a way that he seems to have been utterly ignorant? He very obviously did not know what was meant by those words of Virgil's, 'To what do you not drive mortal hearts, accursed hunger for gold?'—which words have never been doubtful to anyone of even moderate learning—since although they were spoken against avarice, he took them as a curse on prodigality.[11] And he describes Marcus Cato, who perished in the civil wars, as a very old man with a long white beard—an obvious display of ignorance, since he died at Utica in the forty-eighth year of his life and in his prime. However, this is of little weight; what is more serious and intolerable is his damning with the greatest penalty Marcus Brutus, a man distinguished for justice, discretion, magnanimity—in short, for every virtue—because he slew Caesar and plucked from robbers' jaws the liberty of the Roman people. But for driving out a king he placed Junius Brutus in the Elysian Fields. And yet Tarquin had received the kingdom from his forefathers, and was king at a time when the laws permitted that there be a king; whereas Caesar had taken possession of the commonwealth by force of arms, and when the good citizens had been slain he had taken away his country's liberty. Therefore if Marcus is wicked, Junius must necessarily be more wicked; but if Junius is to be praised for driving out a king, why should Marcus not be exalted to heaven for cutting down a tyrant? I shall pass over that which I am ashamed, by Jove, was written by a Christian; because he thought the same punishment should be inflicted on the betrayer of him who troubled the world and on the betrayer of Him who saved it.[12]

11. *Aeneid*, III, 56; *Purg.*, XXII, 40.
12. On Cato, *Purg.*, I, 34. Judas, Marcus Brutus and Cassius are in the jaws of Satan (*Inf.*, XXXIV, 61–67), Junius Brutus in Limbo (*Inf.*, IV, 127).

"But let us lay aside these things which regard religion and speak about those which pertain to our studies. I see that they were so generally unknown to Dante that in truth he evidently read with attention the quodlibets of the brothers and annoying stuff of this sort, but of the books of the gentiles, on which his art especially depended, he had no contact even with those that are left. In short, granted he had every other endowment, he surely lacked Latinity. Will we not be ashamed to call him a poet, and even prefer him to Virgil, when he could not speak Latin? I recently read some letters of his, which he seemed to have written very carefully, for they were in his own hand and signed with his seal. But by Hercules, no one is so uncultivated that it would not shame him to have written so awkwardly. On this account, Coluccio, I shall remove that poet of yours from the number of the lettered and leave him to wool workers, bakers, and the like; for he has spoken in such a way that he seems to have wished to be familiar to this sort of men.

"But enough about Dante. Now let us consider Petrarca, although it does not escape me in what a dangerous position I am, so that I have to fear the attacks of the whole people, whom those splendid bards of yours have attached to themselves by I don't know what nonsense (and there is no other fit appellation for what they divulged to be read). But I shall say freely what I feel, and I beg you not to spread abroad this speech of mine. What, then, if some painter should profess to have a great knowledge of the art, and undertake to paint a theater, and then, having aroused men's expectation that another Apelles or Zeuxis has been born in their times, display pictures ridiculously painted and with distorted features? Would he not seem worthy of everyone's derision? I think so, for he who so impudently has professed to know what he does not know deserves no forbearance. Moreover, what if someone should boast that he had a marvelous skill in the art of music, and then, after proclaiming this constantly and having gathered together a great throng desirous of hearing him, should appear capable of no excellence in his art? Would not everyone depart judging that a man who had made such great claims was ridiculous and worthy of being set to slave labor? Absolutely. Those therefore who cannot fulfill their promises are especially to be disdained. And yet nothing was ever cried up the way Francesco Petrarca announced his *Africa:* there is no book of his, almost no major epistle, in which you will not find that work of his sung. But what happened afterwards? From such great promises was there not born a ridiculous mouse?[13] Is there any friend of his who does not admit it would have been preferable either never to have written that book, or to have condemned it to the flames once it was written? How much, then, ought we to value this poet when everyone agrees that what he claims is his greatest work, the one in which he exerts his full force, harms rather than helps his reputation? See what a difference there is between him and our Virgil: the latter rendered obscure men famous with his song, while Petrarca did his best to cause Africanus, a very famous man, to be forgotten. In addition, Francesco wrote a *Bucolic Song;* he also wrote *Invectives,* so that he would be considered not only a poet but also an orator. But he wrote in such a way that in his bucolics there is nothing that smells of the pastoral or sylvan, and in his orations nothing that does not greatly desire the art of rhetoric.

"I can say the same things about Giovanni Boccaccio, the extent of whose ability is manifest in his every work; but I think I have said enough to cover him as well. For since I have shown the many faults of those who in your judgment and everyone else's much excel him (and anyone who wished

13. Cf. Horace, *Ars Poetica,* 139.

to occupy himself with the matter could point out more),
you can suppose that if I wished to talk about Giovanni,
speech would not fail me. However, that fault is common to
them, that they were of a singular arrogance, and did not
believe there would be anyone who could judge their works;
they thought they would be esteemed by everyone as much as
they approved themselves. And so the one calls himself poet,
the second laureate, and the third bard. Alas, wretches, what
darkness blinds you! By Hercules, I far prefer one letter of
Cicero's and one poem of Virgil's to the whole lot of your
works. Wherefore, Coluccio, let them have for themselves
that glory which you say was procured through them for our
city. For my part I repudiate it, nor do I believe we should
think much of that fame which comes from those with no
discernment."

Smiling in his usual way, Coluccio replied: "How I should
wish, Niccolò, that you were kinder to your fellow citizens;
although I realize there was never anyone so universally
approved that he did not find an opponent. Virgil had his
Evangelus, Terence his Lanuvius.[14] Nevertheless with your
leave I shall say what I feel: those whom I just named seem to
me more tolerable than you, for each of them opposed one
person, not his fellow citizens, whereas you have proceeded to
the point of contention where you attempt alone to overthrow three, and your fellow citizens at that. But time prevents my undertaking their defense and protecting them
from your aspersions; for, as you see, the day is now coming
to an end. And so I am afraid we do not have time to treat
this subject, for no few words are needed in their defense—
not because it is very difficult to respond to your charges, but
because it cannot be done rightly without adding in their

14. See Macrobius, *Sat.*, V, i, 19 ff. for the criticisms of Evangelus; Terence,
Heaut., 22, on Luscius Lanuvinus, the "malevolent poet."

praises, a very difficult thing to do properly, considering the greatness of their merits. And so I shall defer that defense to another more convenient time. For the moment I shall say simply this: you, Niccolò, think whatever you wish about those men. I feel they were furnished with many excellent arts and worthy of the name granted them by universal agreement. At the same time I hold, and shall always hold, that there is nothing which assists our studies as much as disputation; and that if these times have suffered some downfall, we have not on that account been deprived of the possibility of practicing it. Wherefore I shall not cease to encourage you to apply yourself particularly to this practice."

When he had said this, we arose.

BOOK II

The next day, when all of us from the day before had come together (and had been joined by Pietro Sermini,[15] an energetic and very eloquent young friend of Coluccio's), we decided to visit Roberto's gardens. After crossing the Arno we arrived there, observed the gardens and returned to that portico which is behind the vestibule. Coluccio sat down to collect himself for a while, then said to us younger men who were standing around in a circle: "How handsome and magnificent are the buildings of our city! I was put in mind of this, while in the gardens, by those dwellings before our eyes, which belong to the worthy brothers whom I have always esteemed and considered friends along with the whole family of the Pitti. But look, please, at the splendor of the dwellings; behold their delightful charm. And I admire these no more than I do the other elegant buildings which fill this whole city; so that often there comes to my mind what Leonardo

15. Ser Pietro di Ser Lorenzo Sermini succeeded Salutati as chancellor.

said in that speech in which he carefully assembled the praises of Florence. Praising its beauty, he said that 'in magnificence Florence perhaps surpasses all cities of the present day; in elegance, those of the present and of the past.'[16] I think this was very truly spoken by Leonardo; for I do not think Rome or Athens or Syracuse was so elegant, but in that respect are far surpassed by this city of ours."

Pietro replied: "That is true, Coluccio; but Florence excels not simply in this, for we see that it is also distinguished in many other things. I thought so previously on my own; and then when I read that commendation I was confirmed in my opinion. For this all the citizens should be grateful to you, Leonardo; such is the diligence with which you have pursued the praises of this city.

"You praise first the city and its embellishments, then its origin from Roman colonists; in the third place you describe its deeds abroad and at home and wonderfully exalt it in every sort of virtue. But one thing particularly pleased me in that speech: you demonstrate that our party endeavors had a splendid origin and were taken up by this city with proper and perfect right.[17] But you cast great odium upon the Caesarean faction, which is hostile to ours, by relating their crimes and by lamenting the lost liberty of the Roman people."

"It was to be sure necessary for Leonardo," said Coluccio, "once he had undertaken to bestow praise upon this city, to inveigh somewhat against the Caesars themselves." "But I remember reading," replied Pietro, "in Lactantius Firmianus, a very learned and eloquent man, that he wondered

16. The first complete edition of Bruni's *Laudatio* has been published by Hans Baron in *From Petrarch to Leonardo Bruni*, pp. 232–263. The judgment cited by Salutati appears (in not exactly the form quoted here) on p. 235.

17. Florence had long been a Guelph (i.e., anti-imperial) city.

greatly for what reason Caesar is exalted to the skies, since he was the parricide of his fatherland. I think Leonardo followed him."[18] "What need is there," answered Coluccio, "to follow Lactantius, when he has as authorities Cicero and Lucan, very learned and wise men, and when he has read Suetonius? But to speak for myself, I could never be led to believe that Caesar was the parricide of his fatherland. It seems to me that I discussed this matter carefully enough in the book I wrote *On the Tyrant,* where I concluded with good reasons that Caesar did not rule wickedly.[19] And so I shall never think Caesar was a parricide, nor shall I stop exalting him to the skies for the greatness of his deeds. Nevertheless, if I had to exhort my sons to virtue, or ask God for it, I should certainly wish them to resemble Marcellus or Camillus rather than Caesar; for they were not inferior in war, and in addition to this military virtue they had moral purity. I do not know if Caesar did; but those who describe his life say the contrary. Therefore it seems to me that Leonardo served his cause actively by mentioning Caesar's virtues and then adding in suspicion of his faults, so as to recommend his cause to fair-minded listeners. I have no doubt it was then that Florence took up these partisan endeavors, and thus began this legalized plotting. What followed later, when those brave men went forth into Apulia against Manfred to avenge the city (in which battle[20] your family excelled greatly, Roberto), that was not the origin of the parties but their splendid restoration. For at

18. Cf. *Div. Inst.,* I, 15, and *Laudatio,* p. 247. On the controversy over Caesar, see Baron, *The Crisis . . . ,* pp. 66–67.

19. Translated in E. Emerton, *Humanism and Tyranny* (Cambridge, Mass., 1925). Chapter V (pp. 110–116) is entitled "That Dante Was Right in Placing Brutus and Cassius in the Lowest Hell as Traitors of the Deepest Dye."

20. In 1266 the Florentine Guelphs helped Charles of Anjou defeat Manfred at Beneventum.

that time those who felt differently from the will of this people had seized control of the state."

"I am very pleased, Coluccio," said Roberto, "that our family was in that battle and according to the judgment of all fought very bravely for the glory of this city. But since we have mentioned this, and you are readily praising its buildings, magnificence, partisan endeavors and finally the glory it has won in war, I think you will do well if you defend against yesterday's vituperation the learned men whom Florence has produced, for those three poets are by no means the smallest part of this city's glory."

Coluccio replied: "You are right, Roberto: they are not the smallest part of our glory; rather, by far the greatest. But what remains to be done? Yesterday did I not sufficiently set forth my feelings about those great men?" "You did," said Roberto, "but we were waiting for you to respond to the accusations." "What accusations?" said Coluccio. "Who is so clumsy that he could not very easily confute them? I know the defenses against those charges are plain to all of you present; but you wish to be very cunning and crafty. Is there any of you who does not think he can deceive a gray-haired old man? But it is not so, young men, believe me; for a long life is instructive, and from experience has come greater wisdom. Your stratagem did not escape my notice yesterday, Niccolò, when you not only found fault with our poets but even inveighed against them with some sharpness. You believed that I would be roused to leap forth immediately in praise of them; and I think you were in on it with Leonardo, who for some time has been asking me to write their praises. Although I want to do this and comply with Leonardo's wishes, since he daily undertakes for us the task of translating Greek into Latin, nevertheless, Niccolò, I should be unwilling to seem impelled by your deceptions. And so when it pleases me I shall relate the praises of those men; but I shall not do it today, so that your stratagems will not attain their purpose."

Roberto replied: "Since here you are in my realm, Coluccio, I shall never let you depart without first responding to those charges." And Niccolò said with a smile: "Come Roberto, since our stratagems have not been very successful let us assail him by force." Coluccio answered: "Never, by Hercules, will you force me to sing like a caged bird. But if it is dear to your heart, entrust it to Leonardo here: having praised the whole city he should rightfully also praise these men." I answered: "If I were able to do so in accord with their merits, Coluccio, I should be not at all reluctant; but I do not have such power of speech, and I should not dare any such thing in your presence. Therefore either comply with Roberto's wishes, or choose me as an arbiter to settle this controversy between you." When they had all expressed their willingness, I said: "I wish to be seated, so that my judgment will have weight." And at the same time I ordered the others to sit down. This done, I made known my sentence: that Niccolò should now defend the same men he had assailed the day before, while Coluccio listened and criticized.

With a smile Coluccio replied: "Leonardo could not have made a better judgment, for no remedy is more effective than cleansing opposites with opposites." And Niccolò said: "I should have preferred to listen to you, Coluccio; but so long as you understand that I brought to you this matter which I myself do not refuse to undertake (provided I have the speaking ability), I shall not resist this sentence. I shall follow it and obey the decree, and I shall respond in due order to the objections that were made. But first of all be assured that my only reason for attacking yesterday was to stimulate Coluccio to praise them. But it was difficult to make the wisest of men think I was speaking sincerely, not making it up. For he had seen that I was always studious and

always lived among books and letters; he could remember
that I had a singular esteem for those very Florentine poets.
Dante himself at one time I committed to memory so well
that not even today have I forgotten it: even now I can quote
without books a great part of that magnificent and excellent
poem—which I could not do without a singular love for it. I
always esteemed Francesco Petrarca so highly that I went all
the way to Padua to transcribe his books from his own original. In fact, I was the first to bring the *Africa* here, as
Coluccio will testify. And how can I hate Giovanni Boccaccio, I who at my own expense adorned his library to honor
the memory of so great a man, and am in it most frequently
among the eremites?[21] Therefore, as I was just saying, it was
hard to keep Coluccio from perceiving my dissimulation.
Would he ever have thought that I, who had shown such
signs of good will toward those poets, was so changed in one
day that thugs, cobblers and brokers, men who never saw
letters or tasted the sweetness of poetry, valued Dante or
Petrarca or Boccaccio more highly than I, who have always
revered and delighted in them, and have honored their
memory in deed as well as word, after I could no longer see
them? Great indeed would be our ignorance, if men of this
sort were going to deprive us of their poems.

"I say this so that you can perceive what was evident even
without my saying anything: that I censured those very
learned men not because I thought them worthy of censure,
but to incite Coluccio to praise them out of indignation. The
Florentine poets seemed to call, Coluccio, for your genius,
your art of speaking and your knowledge; and this would
have been very agreeable to me. Since you are not willing to
do so at present, I shall try, to the best of my ability, to take
your place; however, any deficiency must be blamed on you
and Leonardo, who have imposed this necessity on me."

21. Niccoli had provided cases in S. Spirito for Boccaccio's books.

"Proceed, Niccolò," said Coluccio, "and do not beg off from this duty any longer." "It seems to me, then," began Niccolò, "that three things are necessary in a great poet: imagination, eloquence and a knowledge of many things. Of these three the first is peculiar to poets, while they have the second in common with the orator and the third with philosophers and historians. Provided these three are present, there is nothing further to be required in a poet. Let us see, then, if it is agreeable to you, of what sort these were in our poets; and let us begin with Dante, who is older. Is there anyone who would dare say that he was deficient in imagination, he who devised such a new and remarkable representation of the three realms, and divided them all in various sections so that the many sins of this world are punished each in its own place according to the magnitude of each? For what am I to say about the *Paradiso?* Its order is so great, it has been described with such care, that so beautiful a representation could never be praised adequately. Moreover what about his descent and ascent, what about those companions and guides, contrived with such elegance? What about the exactness of the hours? For what am I to say about the eloquence which makes all his predecessors look like infants? There are no tropes, no regalia of the art of rhetoric, which are not wonderfully spread through his works, and they have no less embellishment than richness. Mellifluous streams of words flow forth spontaneously and express all his perceptions as if they were placed under the listeners' or readers' eyes. Nor is there any obscurity so great that his discourse does not illumine and explain it; for—most difficult of all—in those polished terzine he relates and discusses the most acute thoughts of theology and philosophy so aptly that it could hardly be done better by theologians and philosophers themselves in the leisure of the school.

"Add to this his incredible knowledge of history. Whether for embellishment or instruction, in this noble work have been joined things old and new, domestic and foreign. In Italy there is no custom, no mountain, no river, no family of any note, no man who had done anything worthy of memory, that has not found a suitable place in his poem. And so what Coluccio was doing yesterday, matching Dante with Virgil and Homer, by no means displeases me; for I know nothing in their poems to which this poem of ours does not offer a full counterpart. Read, please, those verses in which he portrays love, hate, fear and other disturbances of the spirit; read his temporal descriptions, the movements of the heavens, the risings and settings of the stars, the arithmetical computations; read the exhortations, the invectives, the consolations—then ask yourself what any poet could bring forth more perfect in wisdom and more polished in elegance. This man, then, so elegant, so eloquent and so learned, I yesterday removed from the number of the lettered so that he should be not with them but above them, since with his poem he delights not only them but the whole city.

"Now, since I think I have expressed sufficiently what I feel about the citizen, about the poet, about this very learned man, I shall respond to the charges that are made against him. *Marcus Cato died in the forty-eighth year of his life and in his prime; but Dante imagines him with a long white beard.* This charge is groundless; for the souls of the dead, not their bodies, go to the underworld. Why therefore did Dante represent his hair? Because the mind of Cato, who was a strict guardian of virtue and endowed with great moral purity, was very old even in a youthful body. Were we not hearing a while ago how little Coluccio valued youth? And not unjustly; for wisdom belongs to old age, as do soundness of character and temperance, which make for integrity. *But he misunderstood those verses of Virgil's:* 'To what do you not drive mortal hearts, accursed hunger for gold?' I am afraid rather that we do not understand Dante, for of what avail is it to say he did not know what is known even to boys? How could it happen that he who saw through to Virgil's most obscure meanings should be led astray by this obvious verse? It is not so: either it is a fault of the scribes (most of whom are ignorant dolts) , or Virgil's saying has been applied to the other extreme, so that since liberality is a virtue situated between the extremes of avarice and prodigality, two equal vices, when one has been censured the censure is also applied to the other. This deceived Virgil also, who wondered greatly at Statius' having been avaricious, when Statius actually had paid the penalty for prodigality.

"As for the third charge—that *he says just the same punishment is inflicted on him who killed the Savior of the world as on Him who killed its troubler*—it labors from the same fault as the censure concerning Cato's age. Foolish men often make the mistake of taking things said by poets as if they were true, not invented. Do you suppose that Dante, the most learned man of his age, did not know how Caesar had attained power? That he did not know liberty was abolished and a diadem placed on Caesar's head by Mark Antony while the Roman people groaned? Do you think he was ignorant of the great virtue with which all histories agree Brutus had been endowed? For who does not praise that man's justice, integrity, diligence and greatness of spirit? No, Dante was not ignorant of this; but in Caesar he represented the legitimate prince and the just worldly monarch, in Brutus the seditious, trouble-making criminal who sinfully slays this prince—not because Brutus was of this sort, for if he were, on what ground would the Senate have praised him as the recoverer of liberty? But since Caesar had ruled, whatever the manner, and since Brutus together with more than sixty noble citizens had slain him, the poet took from this material for invention. Why therefore did he place in the jaws of Lucifer the best and justest man, the recoverer of liberty? Well, why did

Virgil make a pure woman,[22] who suffered death in order to preserve her chastity, so libidinous that she killed herself for the sake of love? Painters and poets have always had the same ability to dare anything. Though perhaps, to be sure, it could well be maintained that Brutus was impious in slaying Caesar; for there are not lacking authors who—whether on account of good will toward those parties, or to please the emperors—call that deed of Brutus' wicked and impious. But for that matching of Christ and Caesar the first defense seems more probable, and I have no doubt our poet felt so.

"But even if he had all these things, he certainly lacked Latinity. This was said to provoke Coluccio's indignation; for who in his right mind would patiently hear that Dante—who had disputed so often, who wrote heroic poems, who was approved in so many studies—was ignorant of letters? That could in no way happen. Necessarily he was very well versed in letters and learned and eloquent and fitted for imaginative writing—clear proof of which is afforded not only by men's opinions but also by his own writings.

"Now since I have said, I think, enough about Dante, let us say a few things about our Petrarca, although the excellence of such a man would not be satisfied with a few praises. But I beg that you listen to me as to a man insufficiently suited for speaking, especially since, as you all see, I must speak extemporaneously and completely without any consideration beforehand." Pietro replied: "Proceed, Niccolò. We are not unacquainted with your ability, which we have just experienced in your commendation and defence of Dante, for you omitted no topic of praise." Niccolò proceeded: "When, as I said before, I had traveled to Padua to transcribe the books of our Petrarca, not many years after his death, I often met those men who were his good friends while

22. I.e., Dido.

he was alive. From them I obtained such an acquaintance with his character that it was almost as if I had seen him myself—although previously I had heard the same from the very venerable and learned theologian, Luigi. They all, then, declared that in Petrarca there had been many things worthy of praise, but three especially; for they said he had been very handsome, and wise, and the most learned man of his age. All these things they attested with witnesses and reasoned arguments. But let us say nothing of his good looks and wisdom, since they regard his personal life. I do not suppose you have failed to hear of his dignity, moderation, integrity, moral purity and other outstanding virtues; but as I say, let us pass over these as private matters. However, since he left it for us all let us consider his learning and the reasoning by which they showed that our Petrarca excelled in this as well. When they praised his learning, then, they said that Francesco Petrarca was to be set before all the poets who preceded him. Beginning with Ennius and Lucretius they ran on to our own times in such a way that whatever poet they adduced was shown to have been brilliant in some one genre. The work of Ennius, Lucretius, Pacuvius and Accius consisted of poems, but none of them wrote any prose worth being praised. Petrarca, though, left beautiful poems in elegant verse, and many books in prose. So great was his genius that he equaled the best poets with his poetry and the most learned orators with his prose. When they had shown me his poems—heroic, bucolic, familiar—they brought forth as testimony to his prose many books and epistles; they showed me exhortations to virtue, censures of vice, and many things which he wrote about cherishing friendship, about loving one's country, about the ordering of states, about disdaining fortune, about the correction of character. From this it was easy to perceive that he had abundant learning. Moreover, his genius was so accommodated to every type of composition that he did not

refrain from the popular sort of writing; in this, as in the
others, he appears most elegant and eloquent.

"When they had shown me this they asked me if I had
anyone from all antiquity who could prove a match for such
praises, to bring him forward; but if I could not do so, and
had no one equally proficient in every genre, I should not
hesitate to set my fellow citizen before all the most learned
men up to this day.

"I do not know how it seems to you, but I have now
touched upon just about all the points they used to establish
Petrarca's cause. Since their arguments struck me as excellent
I agreed with them and persuaded myself that such was the
case. But will those foreigners think this way, while we are
cooler in praise of our fellow citizen? Shall we not venture to
honor him for his merits, especially when this man restored
liberal studies, which had been extinguished, and opened
the way for us to be able to learn? And perhaps he was the
first to bring the laurel to our city. *But the book to which he
most applied himself is not much approved.* Who is so severe
a critic as not to approve it? I should like him to be asked on
what grounds he does this; although if there were anything in
the book which could be condemned, that would be because
death had prevented Petrarca's polishing it thoroughly. *But
his bucolics have no pastoral flavor.* I do not think so, however; for I see everything stuffed with shepherds and flocks—
when I see you."

When everyone laughed at this, Niccolò added: "I am
speaking because I heard some people making such charges
against Petrarca: don't think I have any part in them. But
since I had heard them from certain people, I repeated them
to you yesterday, for the reason you now know. And so now it
pleases me to rebut not myself—since I was pretending—but
the silly fools who really thought that. What they say, about
preferring one poem of Virgil's and one epistle of Cicero's to

all the works of Petrarca, I often turn around this way: I say that I far prefer an oration of Petrarca's to all the epistles of Virgil, and the poems of Petrarca to all the poems of Cicero.

"But enough, now; let us come to Boccaccio. His learning, eloquence, humor, and especially the excellence of his genius, I admire in every field and in every work. With great eloquence and charm he sang, recounted and wrote the genealogies of the gods, mountains and rivers, the various ends of men, famous women, bucolic poems, loves, nymphs, and infinite other things. Who therefore would not love him? Who would not consider all these poets the greatest part of our city's glory?

"This, then, is what I had to say about our renowned poets; speaking in the presence of learned men, I have passed over some minor points. Now, Coluccio, since you promise you are going to do it, I accordingly ask you, without any (as you were saying a while ago) deception, to support these outstanding men and honor them with your eloquence." "But," replied Coluccio, "I do not see that you have left anything which could be added to their praises." Then Pietro said: "I have at all times admired your speaking ability, Niccolò, and today especially. You have managed a cause to which scarcely any approach seemed left to you in such a way that it could not be argued better or more elegantly. Wherefore, if we have been your judges, since we have been ordered to sit and hear your cause, in my judgment you are absolved; and as I have always deemed you a good and learned man, I deem you thus now, especially since your virtue has been thoroughly beheld and known. You have carefully learned Dante's poem; for love of Petrarca you went all the way to Padua; and out of affection for Boccaccio you embellished his library at your own expense. Leaving aside all other things you have given yourself to literary studies; you are so well versed in Cicero, Pliny, Varro, Livy—in short, all those ancients who make the Latin language renowned—that all men who know anything admire you greatly."

"For my part," replied Niccolò, "I am amply rewarded by finding such praises in so eloquent a mouth. But please, Pietro, more moderation, especially since I in no way deceive myself—I know well enough who I am and what ability there is in me. When I read those ancients whom you just mentioned (which I do as much as possible), when I consider their wisdom and eloquence, I am so far from supposing that I know anything—recognizing, as I do, the dullness of my own genius—that it seems not even the greatest geniuses can learn anything at this time. But the more difficult I think it, the more I admire the Florentine poets, who against the opposition of the times nevertheless by some superabundance of genius managed to equal or surpass those ancients." Roberto said: "The night has returned you to us, Niccolò; for the sort of thing you were saying yesterday was clearly at variance with our company." "Yesterday," Niccolò replied, "I had determined to acquire your books; for I know that if I had persuaded you, you would have auctioned them off at once." At this point Coluccio said: "Roberto, order the doors to be opened, for we can now go forth without fear of calumny." Answered Roberto: "I shall not do so unless you first promise me . . . " "What?" said Coluccio. "That you will all dine with me tomorrow; for I have something I wish celebrated with a convivial discussion." "These three," replied Coluccio, "were going to dine with me; therefore you will offer a meal not to them, but to me." "As you please," answered Roberto, "provided you come." "We shall come," said Coluccio, "if I may answer for my guests. But prepare a twofold banquet—one by which our bodies, the other by which our spirits may be refreshed."

This said, we returned, Roberto accompanying us as far as the Ponte Vecchio.

4

Francesco Filelfo

IN PRAISE OF DANTE[1]

O most eminent and noble citizens, were the bright radiance of man's soul not impeded by its bodily instrument, surely it would never be obscured by any shadows of ignorance. Instead, as the grave philosopher Xenocrates has most sagely shown, it would know every truth in its perfection. Yet since mortals' souls are shut into this weak and disgustingly evil body as into a dark and shadowy prison, we are all in common subject to ignorance. Not without reason, then, would the prudent Academicians reprove those who ardently desired to affirm something as true; for if truth is the object of wisdom, as the learned Plutarch labors to prove by very subtle argument, and if all other virtues are subject to the rule of wisdom alone, then it is quite clear that whoever affirms the truth is evidently a wise man and hence not deprived of any lofty and magnificent virtue. In how much foolishness that man abounds, Socrates demonstrated: after having been judged the wisest by the oracle of Apollo, he used to respond with great urbanity that the judgment was correct, for although every other man considered himself wise and understanding, yet he knew only one thing—that he knew nothing.[2]

1. Translated from *Due Orazioni di Francesco Filelfo in Lode dello Illustrissimo Poeta Dante Alighieri*, Michele Dello Russo, ed. (Naples, 1867).
2. Cf. Plato, *Apology*, 21, a–d.

Although no one is or ought to think himself wise, yet one person is less oppressed by ignorance than another. This comes about in part by the better composition and temper of our bodies and in part by our diligence and industriousness, which can easily aid and remedy every natural defect. Demosthenes and Cicero were by nature slow and tiresome speakers; and yet what man has ever had such fluency, such capacity for embellishments, such elegance, such facility; who could compare in the slightest way to the suavity, the fullness and splendor of their incredible and almost divine eloquence? An expert physiognomist once judged Socrates, of whom we just spoke, to be very depraved by nature; and yet even to the present day everyone has held him to be the father and prince of philosophers, no less for the continence, integrity and sanctity of his life than for his wondrous and varied learning. Yet these same people who achieved good and laudable works by their diligence possessed imbalances and faults not otherwise than did Alcibiades, Lucius Catiline, Publius and Claudius and Mark Anthony, who achieved flagitious and evil ends by overcoming and repressing the favorable tendencies of their nature through desire and negligence.

Surely he may be called happy and blessed in whom the disposition of his bodily parts corresponds to his desire and well-being. Of such perfection among the ancients are numbered few if any save Pythagoras of Samos, Plato, Xenophon the Socratic, and Julius Caesar. And what shall we say of the last century? We shall say nothing of the present, but was that last century not fortunate? Certainly the celestial influences were most benign to it, most prosperous for it, most favorable to it, for we see that in those times nature and divine prudence produced a spirit to whose perfection nothing is lacking. Who was this man? He was the noble and illustrious poet Dante Alighieri. I cannot easily tell whether the singular greatness and unheard-of glory of his marvelous

eloquence, immortal wisdom and divine genius was due more
to nature or to industry. In truth Dante was so pre-eminent
and miraculously gifted by way of both that I would not in
my judgment dare to advance any of the ancients over him. I
doubt anyone can deny me one thing—never has there been
any other writer in the Italian tongue from whom, above and
beyond the melodious harmony of his divine poem, every
man may draw utility in a more universal fashion. And what
utility may we obtain from his poem? That of which no other
is greater, more pleasing, or more sublime. What could
possibly be more welcome, more fruitful, more necessary,
more happy than to recognize virtue with its longed-for
rewards, to know God to whom, as to our sole and ultimate
good, we must direct all our work, all our counsel, all our
intention and thought, just as Aristotle describes with his
lofty erudition and gravity?

Thus every art and every doctrine, like each human act
and choice, hungers and searches for a certain particular good
as its chief and necessary end. And all the particular goods are
desired not so much in themselves as in order to obtain that
highest and ultimate happy state. How much the more must
we Christians not only struggle in civic life, but also in firm
and serious contemplation desire to know and understand
what may be those particular goods by which, as by steps and
terraces, we may ascend and arrive at that ultimate, even to
that uniquely true, perpetual and sempiternal good, to the
principle and glory of which are universally subjected all
immortal and supernal things just as the lower and fallen
things. Alas, how foolish we are, how unfortunate and miserable! Blinded by the passions, we have abandoned reason, the
guide and leader of our life; and we serve nothing else but
our vain appetites, our bodily pleasures and sordid delights.
We have forgotten that divine and supremely wise teaching
that was written in the temple of Phoebus at Delphi, *know*

thy self, which means know your soul, know the mortality and weakness of the body, know the eternal torments, and be troubled by the villainous and impious life; know the immortal and sempiternal rewards of laudable and glorious works.

So then, most excellent citizens, our eminent and illustrious poet Dante having written of these matters with his most sweet and mellifluous eloquence, his sharp and perspicacious wit, his incomparable and almost unheard-of learning, I, after having searched for what would be no less useful than welcome to you, have found him alone to deserve the hearing of your most grave and wise judgment.

If by chance I have done less than satisfy your opinion with this exposition and lecture, I am most certain that in your rare humanity you shall blame not my faultless will and devotion toward your excellencies, but rather the difficulty of the subject and the foolishness and weakness of my poor talent and learning.

5

LEONARDO BRUNI

LIFE OF DANTE[1]

After my having finished recently a rather long work, there came to me the desire to read something in the vernacular tongue, in order to refresh my tired mind. For as at the dining table a single food, so in studies the same reading continued becomes displeasing. While I was searching with this intent, there came into my hands a small work of Boccaccio entitled *Della vita, costumi, e studi del chiarissimo poeta Dante*; and although I had read it diligently before, yet this time in examining it again I thought that our Boccaccio, delightful and agreeable man that he is, had nonetheless written the life and customs of the sublime poet as if he had been writing the *Filocolo,* or the *Filostrato,* or the *Fiammetta.* For it is full of love and sighs and burning tears; it is as if man were born into this world only to find himself in those ten days of love which enamored ladies and charming young men told of in the *Hundred Tales.*[2] And he is so

---

1. Translated from Angelo Solerti, *Le vite di Dante, Petrarca e Boccaccio scritte fino al secolo decimosesto* (Milan, 1904). The following Bruni texts are also in this volume.

2. *Hundred Tales,* i.e., the *Decameron,* ten tales of which are told on each of ten successive days. Boccaccio's *Filocolo, Filostrato* and *Fiammetta* are heavily romantic medieval texts, the first stemming from the Breton-French prose romances, the second from the *Roman de Troie* of Benoît de Sainte-Maure. His biography of Dante has been known by various titles, but now is generally referred to as the *Trattatello in laude di Dante.*

enflamed in these parts concerning love that the grave and important parts of Dante's life are left behind and passed over in silence. The delightful little things are remembered and concerning the serious ones there is only silence. I then proposed for my recreation to write the life of Dante anew, with greater notice given to more valuable things. I do not do this to detract from Boccaccio, but in order as it were that my writings should supplement his. And I shall then add the life of Petrarca, since the fame of these two poets, I maintain, belongs in great part to the glory of our city. We come then first to the life of Dante.

Dante's ancestors were Florentine, of a very old family—and he seems to imply in certain places that they were of those Romans who founded Florence.[3] But this is a very uncertain point, and according to my opinion nothing but guesswork. Yet of those whom we know something about, his great-great-grandfather was the Florentine knight Cacciaguida, of the emperor Conrad's army.[4] Cacciaguida had two brothers, one named Moronto, the other Eliseo. We read of no descendants of Moronto, but from Eliseo was born the family called the Elisei, and perhaps they had this name earlier. From Cacciaguida was born the family of the Alleghieri, called by this name from one of his sons whose mother's family was named Aldighieri. Cacciaguida, his brothers, and their ancestors lived just into the area of Porta San Piero,[5] where one used to enter from the Old Market, in the houses which still today are called those of the Elisei, because they were theirs in antiquity. Cacciaguida's descen-

3. The Roman founding of Florence has been shown to be an important conception in Bruni's thought by Hans Baron. See *The Crisis* . . . , pp. 61–64, and passim. Cf. *Inf.*, XV, 76–78.

4. Cf. *Parad.*, XV, 88–96, 136–141, XVI, 34–42. Nothing else is known of Cacciaguida.

5. Porta San Piero was on the east side of the center of Florence, now the intersection of Via del Proconsolo and the Corso.

dants named the Alleghieri lived on the square behind San Martino del Vescovo, opposite the street that goes to the house of the Sacchetti; and on the other side they were close to the houses of the Donati and the Giuochi.

Dante was born in the year A.D. 1265, shortly after the return to Florence of the Guelphs, who had been exiled for the defeat at Monte Aperto.[6] In his childhood he was liberally raised and given to the preceptors of letters; very soon he showed great genius and much capability for excellent things. He lost his father Aldighieri in his boyhood; nonetheless, comforted by his household and by Brunetto Latini, a very worthy man in the judgment of those times, he gave himself not only to literature but also to the other liberal studies, leaving nothing behind that pertains to the growth of an excellent man. And for all this, he did not close himself up in studious leisure or separate himself from his times, but living and talking with his contemporaries he found himself well adapted and aware and hardy in all youthful activities. In that memorable and great battle fought at Campaldino,[7] the young and highly regarded Dante fought vigorously on horseback in the first rank, which was very dangerous. For the first battle was between cavalry troops, in which the knights of the party from Arezzo beat the Florentine knights with great misfortune to them, who had to flee scattered and defeated to their own lines of foot soldiers. It was this rout that lost the battle for the Aretini,[8] since their victorious knights pursued those in flight for a great distance, and left their own foot soldiers behind. Thus from this moment forth they were fighting in no single place, but rather with the

6. I.e., Montaperti, a few miles east of Siena, where on September 4, 1260, the Florentine Guelphs were thoroughly defeated by the Ghibelline coalition.
7. Between Poppi and Bibbiena in the Casentino, the Florentine Guelphs defeated the Ghibellines from Arezzo, June 11, 1289.
8. I.e., those of Arezzo.

knights alone without aid of the foot soldiers and the foot soldiers then by themselves without aid from the knights. And on the Florentine side, the opposite occurred, for by the retreat of the knights to the infantry lines, they all became one body and easily defeated first the knights and then the foot soldiers. Dante recounts this battle in one of his epistles,[9] and says that he was there in the fighting and he sketches the form of the battle; to understand it, we must know that the Uberti, Lamberti, Abati, and all the others who had left Florence were with the Aretini; and all those who had left Arezzo, the Guelph nobles and people who in that time had all been exiled, were with the Florentines. This is the reason that the words written in the palace say "When the Ghibellines were defeated at Certomondo" and not "the Aretini," so that the party from Arezzo which was with the Commune in the victory should take no offense. Returning to our subject, I say that Dante fought valorously for his native land in this battle, and I wish that our Boccaccio had mentioned this valor rather than the nine years of love, and similar trifles, which because of his account are told of so great a man. But what good is saying it? The tongue goes all the same to the tooth that hurts, and the man who likes to drink always talks of wine.

After this battle, Dante returned home and gave himself over to studies even more than before. Nonetheless, he left aside nothing of cultural and civil affairs. It is a marvelous thing that although he was studying continuously, yet it would never have seemed to anyone that he studied, because of his pleasant habits and youthful conversation. On this point I am happy to correct the error of many ignorant people who believe that there is no student who does not

9. Bruni's remark here is the only notice of such a letter. See Paget Toynbee, *Dantis Alagherii Epistolae* (Oxford, 1966), p. xx.

hide himself away in solitude and leisure. I have never seen any one of those who are hidden away and removed from conversation with men who knew three languages. The great and lofty intellect does not need such torments; rather, it is most certainly the correct conclusion that he who does not learn soon will never learn at all. Thus to estrange oneself from conversation is characteristic of those who with their low intellects are not adapted to learning anything.

Dante not only participated in civil conversation with other men, he also took a wife in his youth. She was a gentlewoman of the Donati family, called Monna Gemma, from whom he had several children, as we shall note in another part of this work. Here Boccaccio loses his patience and says that having a wife is contrary to the studious life: he does not remember that Socrates, the greatest philosopher there ever was, had a wife and children and held offices in the republic of his city; and that Aristotle, who is unsurpassed in wisdom and learning, had two wives at different times and had plenty of children and riches. And Marcus Tullius, Cato, Seneca, and Varro, all great Latin philosophers, had wives and children and carried out offices and duties in the Republic. May Boccaccio pardon me—his opinions are very frivolous on this topic, and very distant from the correct judgment. Man is a social animal, according to what the philosophers say. His first joining, from the multiplication of which is born the city, is husband and wife, and nothing can be perfect where this is lacking, for only this love is natural, legitimate and permissible.

Dante, having taken a wife and living his honest and studious life in society, was frequently employed in affairs of the Republic. And finally when he reached the necessary age he was created one of the priors, not by lot as we do today but by election as was the custom in those times. In the office of the priory with him were Palmieri Altoviti, Neri the son of

Jacopo degli Alberti, and other colleagues. This term was in the year 1300. From this period of office derived his exile and all the adversity of his life, according to what he wrote in an epistle which reads as follows:

All my ill and troubles had their cause and origin in the unfortunate meetings during my term as prior, of which although for my prudence I was not worthy nonetheless for my good faith and my age I was not unworthy, since ten years had already passed since the battle of Campaldino in which the Ghibelline party was almost entirely killed and undone; I went there not a boy in arms and there I experienced much fear and finally great joy over the various developments of the battle.

These are his words.[10] Now the reason for his exile I want to speak of in particular, since it is a noteworthy thing, and Boccaccio passes over it dryshod—for perhaps he did not know about it, as we do from the history we have written.[11]

The city of Florence, after having gone through much division between the Guelphs and the Ghibellines, finally rested in the hands of the Guelphs. In this state it remained for a considerable length of time, until there came another curse of factionalism within the ranks of the Guelphs who were ruling the Republic. The parties were called the Whites and the Blacks. This perverse development first arose among the Pistoians, and above all in the family of the Cancellieri. When Pistoia was already divided, the Florentines in trying to remedy the situation ruled that the leaders of these sects should come to Florence, so that they would make no more trouble there. This solution of removing the leaders brought less good to the Pistoians than evil to the Florentines, who

10. Cf. preceding footnote. Toynbee, p. xx, takes this passage as indicating another lost letter.
11. Bruni's *Historiae Florentini Populi* is considered the ranking work of early humanist historiography: see Baron, *The Crisis* . . . , Part One: "Changes in Politics and Historical Thought."

brought this pestilence upon themselves. For the leaders, variously aided by a number of relatives and friends whom they had in Florence, soon lit the flame of a greater conflagration than that which they had left in Pistoia. They busied themselves with this matter both in public and in private, and the bad seed spread miraculously. The entire city became divided in such a way that there was hardly a family, whether noble or plebeian, which was not divided within itself, nor was there a man of any note who was not of one sect or the other. In many cases the division came even between brothers, one holding to this side, the other to that.

After the contention had lasted several months and the troubles had multiplied not only in words but also in contemptible and bitter deeds, which began first among the young and proceeded then among men of maturity, the whole city was full of rebellion and suspicion. While Dante was one of the priors, it happened that a certain meeting was held by the Blacks in the Church of Santa Trinita; what it concerned was held tightly secret, but the general idea was to work with Pope Boniface VIII, who was then in the See, so that he might send Charles of Valois, of the kings of France, to pacify and reform the city of Florence. When the other side heard of this meeting, they quickly became very suspicious; they took up arms, banded together with their friends, and went to the priors, to whom they complained about the assembly and its having taken counsel in private of the state of the city; and all this was done, they said, in order to exile them from Florence. On that account, they asked the priors to punish such a presumptuous outrage. Those who had assembled were also afraid: they took up arms and complained to the priors of their adversaries, who without public deliberation had armed and fortified themselves, and they claimed on various pretexts that the others wanted to exile them. They asked the priors to punish them for disturbing the public order. The one part and the other had provided themselves with soldiers and friends. The fear and terror and danger were tremendous. With the city then at arms and deep in troubles, the priors, following Dante's counsel, saw to the defending of themselves from the people. And when they had fortified themselves, they sent to the borders the leaders of the two sects, who were the following: Corso Donati, Geri Spini, Giacchinotto de' Pazzi, Rosso della Tosa, and others. All these were of the Black party, and were banished to Castel della Pieve in the area of Perugia. Of the White party, the following were exiled to Serezzana: Gentile and Torrigiano de' Cerchi, Guido Cavalcanti, Baschiera della Tosa, Baldinaccio Adimari, Naldo son of Lottino Gherardini, and others.

All this weighed heavily on Dante. Despite his excuses of being a man of no party, he was nonetheless thought to tend toward the Whites and to have been displeased, considering it scandalous and troublesome for the city, that the council should have been held to call Charles of Valois to Florence. The ill will then increased, because that part of the citizens who were confined at Serezzana quickly returned to Florence, while the other part, confined at Castel della Pieve, remained in exile. Dante replied to this point that when those of Serezzana were called back, he was out of office and that he should not be held responsible for it. Furthermore, he said that they had returned because of the illness and death of Guido Cavalcanti, who became sick at Serezzana because of the climate and died shortly thereafter.[12] This imbalance moved the Pope to send Charles of Valois to Florence, who was received into the city by reverence for the Pope and for the House of France; he brought back the exiled citizens, and shortly thereafter banished the White party because of the

12. Toynbee, p. xxi, assumes another lost letter. Cf. notes 9 and 10 above.

revelations of a certain treatise set out by Piero Ferranti, one of his barons. Ferranti said that he had been asked by three gentlemen of the White party, namely, Naldo son of Lottino Gherardini, Baschiera della Tosa and Baldinaccio Adimari, to arrange with Charles of Valois that their party should remain superior in the land and that they had promised to give him the governing of Prato in return, if he did this. And he produced this request and promise in writing with the seals of the above-named men. I have seen the original writing, for it is still today in the palace among other public documents; but in my opinion, it seems very suspect and I think it was created out of whole cloth. Yet be that as it may, there followed the exile of the entire White party, since Charles reacted with scorn to their request and promise.

At this time Dante was not in Florence but in Rome, having been sent there shortly before as ambassador to the Pope in order to offer the agreement and peace of his citizens. Nonetheless, in the anger of those who had been exiled during his term as prior, his house was sacked by the Black party and all his possessions were stolen and destroyed. Both he and Palmieri Altoviti were banished for the default of not appearing, not for the fact of any deed committed. They brought about the banishment in this way: they enacted a perverse and iniquitous law, effective retroactively, that the Podestà of Florence could and should recognize all faults committed by his predecessor in the office of prior, despite pardon that may have been given; Dante was cited according to this law by Conte de' Gabrielli, who was then Podestà of Florence; and since he was absent and did not appear, he was found guilty and exiled, and his possessions were legally confiscated, despite the fact that they had already been stolen and destroyed. We have discussed how Dante's banishment came about, both how and why; now we shall speak of his life in exile.

When Dante heard of his ruin, he quickly left Rome where he had been ambassador, and traveling swiftly he came to Siena. There he clearly understood the nature of the calamity and seeing no recourse he decided to join with the others who had been exiled. He first joined them at Gargonsa, where they assembled and spoke together of many things and finally set up their residence in Arezzo. Here they established a large settlement and created Count Alessandro da Romena their leader, along with twelve counsellors, of whom Dante was one. Here they stayed, passing from one moment of hoping to another, until the year 1304. Then they assembled a great force of all their sympathizers and came to Florence with a great multitude of others, who joined them not only from Arezzo but also from Bologna and Pistoia. Arriving unexpectedly and suddenly, they overcame one of the gates to Florence and won a part of the land. But finally they had to leave without success.

When this great hope of theirs had failed, Dante thought it best not to waste any more time; he left Arezzo and went to Verona, where he was received in a very courteous fashion by the noble della Scala family. He resided there for some time, retiring there in all humility. He tried with good works and good behavior to win the favor that would allow him to return to Florence by a spontaneous revocation of the law by the Florentine governor. To this end he worked a great deal and wrote many times not only to individual citizens but also to the people of Florence at large. Among others there is a rather long epistle which begins "My people, what have I done to you?"[13] While Dante was hoping to return by way of a pardon, there came the election of Henry of Luxembourg

13. Again, the letter is not known today; see Toynbee, pp. xxii–xxiii. The line cited quotes Micah, vi, 3. Concerning Henry, see Dante's *Epistle* VII, addressed "To the most glorious and most fortunate conqueror and sole lord, Lord Henry, by divine providence King of the Romans."

as emperor. Because of this election, first, and second because of his passing through the country, all Italy rose in hope of great new things. Thus Dante could not maintain his proposition of waiting for favor, but rose up in his proud spirit and began to speak ill of those who were ruling the land, calling them villainous and evil and menacing them with their due punishment through the power of the emperor, against whom he said they evidently had no refuge.[14] And yet he held such respect for his native land that when the emperor came up against Florence and camped near the gate, he did not want to be there, as he writes,[15] even though he had supported his coming. Then Henry died during the following summer at Buonconvento, and Dante entirely lost all hope, since he himself had closed the way of a change of favor by having spoken and written against the citizens who were governing the Republic, and there remained no force to support his desires. Thus, having put aside all hope, he passed the rest of his life in poverty, living in various places in Lombardy and Tuscany and the Romagna, with the support of various lords. Finally he retired to Ravenna, where he lived out the remainder of his life.

Now that we have spoken of Dante's public affairs and work, and have shown the course of his life in this respect, we shall speak of his domestic life and of his character and studies.

Although he was not very rich before his exile from Florence, Dante nonetheless was not poor, but had a moderate inheritance sufficient for his living honorably. He had a brother named Francesco Alighieri; and as we have said above, he had a wife and children, from whom there continues today the succession and the family, as we shall men-

---

14. This is *Epistle* VI.
15. No such passage survives in Dante's letters.

tion below. He had an adequate house in Florence, adjacent
to those of Geri di Bello his relative;[16] he had possessions in
addition at Camerata, in the Piacentina and at Piano di
Ripoli, and according to his writings he had abundant and
precious furnishings.[17] He was a very neat man of modest
stature and of agreeable and serious appearance. Although he
spoke slowly and infrequently, his replies were very precise.
His own likeness is seen in the Church of Santa Croce, almost
in the middle of the church, on the left side going toward the
great altar; it was excellently drawn in a natural style by an
excellent artist of his time. Music and sounds delighted
Dante and he did drawings with distinction. Furthermore, he
was a perfect writer, his letters thin and long and very
accurate, as I have seen in several epistles written in his own
hand. In his youth, he was one of the young men in love, yet
he was involved in such a passion not libidinously but
through his gentleness of heart. And he began to write verses
of love in his youthful years, as we can see in one of his
vernacular works, called the *Vita Nuova*. His principal study
was poetry, but it was not of the sterile, impoverished or
fantastic kind; his poetry was fecund and enriched, built
upon true knowledge and great learning.

In order that the reader may understand me better, let me
say that one may become a poet in two ways. One is through
the incitement and motion of personal genius by some inner
and hidden force, which is called *"furor"* and having one's
mind possessed. I will give an analogy to what I mean: the
blessed Francis, not through knowledge or scholastic discipline but through possession and mental detachment, applied his mind to God so strongly that he was transported
beyond human sense, and knew God more than the theolo-

16. Geri (Ruggiero) del Bello degli Alighieri, grandson of the first Alighieri and first cousin of Dante's father.

17. This text, presumably a letter, does not survive.

gians know him by study and books. Thus in poetry one may become a poet through inner incitement and application of the mind, and this is the highest and most perfect kind of poetry. Whoever speaks of poets as divine, and whoever calls them sacred, and whoever calls them seers (*vates*) names them according to this possession and furor. We have examples in Orpheus and Hesiod, of whom both the one and the other were of that kind I have just described. Orpheus had such strength that he moved the stones and the forests with his lyre; and Hesiod, although a coarse and unlearned shepherd, only had to drink from the water of the Castalian spring to become a supreme poet without other studies. We have his works still today, and they are such that none of the literate and learned poets excels him. There is, then, one sort of poet through internal possession and agitation of mind; the other sort comes through knowledge and study, through learning and art and prudence, and Dante was of this second sort. For he acquired the knowledge which he was to adorn and exemplify in his verses through attentive and laborious study of philosophy, theology, astrology, arithmetic, through the reading of history and through the turning over of many different books.

Since we have spoken of the qualities of poets, now we shall speak of the name, by which one will also understand the substance; even though these things can only be said poorly in the vulgar tongue, yet I shall exert myself to offer them to be understood, because in my opinion these modern poets of ours have not understood it well—but that is not surprising since they are ignorant of Greek. I say then that this name of poet is a Greek word and means "maker." From what has been said to this point I know that my words will not be understood, since it is necessary to open the mind further. I say then that some men are readers of others' books and works of poetry, and they do nothing themselves, as happens with most men; other men are makers of these works, as Virgil made the book of the *Aeneid,* and Statius made the book of the *Thebaid,* and Ovid made the book *The Metamorphoses,* and Homer made the *Iliad* and the *Odyssey.* These then who made the works were poets, that is to say, makers of these works which we read. We are readers and they were the makers. And when we hear some worthy man praised for study and learning, we usually ask, "Has he done anything himself? Will he leave behind any work that is composed and made by himself?" The poet then is he who makes any work, that is to say, the author and composer of what others read. Someone might say at this point that according to what I have said, the merchant who writes down his accounts and makes a book of them would be a poet; and Livy and Sallust would be poets since each of them wrote books and works to be read. I reply to this that we do not speak of "making" a work except in verse: this comes about by the excellence of one's studies,[18] since syllables and meter and sound pertain only to writing in verse. We usually say in our vernacular tongue: "He makes songs and sonnets." But when someone writes a letter to his friends, we would not say that he had "made" any work. The name of poet means an excellent and admirable style in verse, covered over and shaded with gaiety and high fiction. As every president commands [*impera*] and rules but we only call emperor [*imperadore*] the greatest of all, so we call poet only the man who composes works in verse and is supreme and most excellent in composing such works. Writing in literary or vernacular style has nothing to do with the case, any more than the difference between writing in Greek or in Latin.

Each language has its own perfection and its own sound, and its polished and learned diction. Yet if someone should

18. Solerti reads "studies": an alternative reading is "style," which seems perhaps preferable given the third sentence following, "The name of poet means an excellent and admirable style. . . ."

ask me why Dante chose to write in the vernacular rather than in Latin and the literate style, I would reply that the truth is right there, that is to say, that Dante knew himself much better adapted to this vernacular style in rhyme than to that Latin and literate style. Certainly he says many things graciously in this vulgar rhyme, which he could not have said and would not have known how to say in Latin and in heroic verses. The proof of this is his *Eclogues,* done in hexameters; agreed they are beautiful, but nonetheless we have seen many that are better written. To speak the truth, the virtue of our poet was in vernacular rhyme, in which he is more excellent than any other; but in Latin verse, or in prose, he barely comes up to the average. The reason for this is that his century was given to rhymed speaking; the men of that time understood nothing of speaking in prose, or in Latin verse, for they were coarse and heavy and unskilled in letters, even if nonetheless learned in these disciplines according to the monkish scholastic manner.

According to Dante, people began to write in rhyme 150 years before him. The first to do so in Italy were Guido Guinizelli of Bologna, the knight Guittone Gaudente d'Arezzo, Buonagiunta da Lucca and Guido da Messina,[19] all of whom Dante surpassed greatly in meaning and polish, in elegance and gaiety, so that it is the opinion of those who understand that no one will ever excel Dante in rhymed poetry. The greatness and sweetness of his poetry is truly marvelous; it is prudent, meaningful and serious, in which there is marvelous fullness and variety, philosophical knowl-

19. Guido Guinizelli (*ca.* 1230–1276) broke from following Guittone d'Arezzo, was then leader of a Bolognese school of poets and became known as the founder of the *dolce stil novo.* Cf. *Purg.,* XI, 97–98, and XXVI, 92–132. Guittone d'Arezzo (*ca.* 1230–1294) , member of the order of Frati Godenti, which included married men and women, was a predecessor of the *dolce stil novo.* Cf. *Purg.,* XXIV, 56–57, XXVI, 124. Buonagiunta da Lucca, notary and poet of the later thirteenth century, followed the Provençal poets. Cf. *Purg.,* XXIV, 19 ff. Guido da Messina (Guido delle Colonne, d. 1257) was a judge at Messina and poet of the Sicilian school.

edge, details of ancient histories and so much understanding
of modern things that he seems to have been present at every
event. These fine things, set out with nobility of rhyme, take
over the mind of the reader, and all the more so the more the
readers understand. His fiction was marvelous, and invented
with great genius; for in it come together description of the
world, description of the heavens and planets, description of
men, of the rewards and punishments of human life, happiness, misery, and the mean of life between the two extremes.
Nor do I think there was ever anyone who learned more
ample and fertile material to be able to explain the sense of
his every thought, through the variety of spirits speaking
about various senses of things, of various lands, and of various
incidents of fortune.

Dante began his principal work before his banishment,
and then finished it in exile, as one can clearly see in that
work. He also wrote moral canzoni and sonnets; the canzoni
are perfect, polished and gay, and full of high thoughts, and
all of them have lavish beginnings. So in that canzone
which begins:

> Amore che muovi tua virtù dal cielo,
> Come il sol lo splendore
> (Love, who move your virtue from the heaven,
> As the sun its splendor)

he makes a philosophical and subtle comparison between the
effects of the sun and the effects of love. Another begins:

> Tre donne intorno al cor mi son venute
> (Three ladies have come round about my heart)

and another[20]

20. *Vita Nuova*, II, cap. xix.

Donne che avete intelletto d'amore
(You ladies who understand love)

and so too in many other canzoni he is subtle and polished
and learned. In the sonnets he is not so forceful. These are
his works in the vernacular.

In Latin he wrote in prose and in verse. In prose he composed a book called the *Monarchy,* written in an unadorned
manner without any nobility of language. He also wrote
another book entitled *De Vulgari Eloquentia.* And he wrote
many prose epistles. In verse he wrote some *Eclogues,* and the
beginning of a book in heroic verses, but not succeeding with
the style, he did not pursue it.

Dante died in 1321 in Ravenna. Among others, Dante had
a son named Piero, who studied law and became a worthy
man; by his own strength and in memory of his father he
made himself a great man, earned a good deal, and settled in
Verona with considerable wealth. Piero had a son named
Dante, and from him was born Leonardo, who is alive today
and has several children. Not long ago Leonardo came to
Florence with other young men from Verona and all bore
themselves well and honorably. He came to visit me, as a
friend in the memory of his great-grandfather Dante. I
showed him the houses of Dante and of his ancestors, and
gave him accounts of many things he did not know, since he
and his family had been estranged from the land. And so it is
that Fortune turns this world, and changes the inhabitants
with the rolling of her wheels.

LIFE OF PETRARCA

Francesco Petrarca, a man of great genius and no less virtue, was born at Arezzo in the Borgo dell'Orto, shortly before sunrise on the twenty-first of July, 1304. The name of his father was Petracolo; his grandfather was named Parenzo; they were originally from Ancisa. Petracolo, the father, lived in Florence and was very active in the Republic: he was sent out as an ambassador of the city on many very serious occasions, often he was employed with other duties of great importance, and in the court he was for a time a scribe of the Riformagioni.[1] He was a worthy man, active and quite prudent.

In that disaster suffered by the Florentine citizenry, when there came the division between Whites and Blacks, this man was believed to sympathize with the White party and consequently was driven from Florence along with the others. Thus he was reduced to living in Arezzo where he stayed, vigorously aiding his party and his faction according to his hope of returning home. Then when his hopes lessened, he left Arezzo and went to the Roman court, which was newly transferred in those times to Avignon.[2] In the court he was well employed with considerable honor and income. There

1. Part of the Florentine government.
2. The family moved to Avignon in 1312, to the court of the French Pope Clement V.

he brought up two sons, one named Gherardo and the other Checco, who was then called Petrarca as we shall observe in this biography.

Petrarca, then, was raised at Avignon and as he began to grow up he showed a gravity of manner and high intellect. He was very attractive in appearance, and his handsomeness lasted throughout his life. After learning letters and finishing his first childhood studies, he gave himself over to the study of civil law, according to the orders of his father. In these studies he persevered several years, but he considered this material too low for his aptitude, for his nature was drawn to higher things and did not much esteem the law and litigation. Secretly he directed all his study to Cicero, to Virgil and Seneca, to Lactantius and to other philosophers, poets and historians. He was already set to write prose, ready for sonnets and edifying canzoni; gentle and gracious in all his speech, he despised the law and its tedious and gross explanatory glossing. He did not pursue the law, and even if the law had pursued him, he would not have accepted it, had his reverence for his father not held him to it.

After the death of his father he became his own master and dedicated himself openly and entirely to those studies of which he had earlier been a disciple in secret for fear of his father. Quickly his fame began to spread; he came to be called not Francesco Petracchi, but Francesco Petrarca, his name made greater out of respect for his virtues. He had such grace of intellect that he was the first to bring back into the light of understanding the sublime studies, so long fallen and ignored. Having grown since then, they have reached their present heights, of which I want to tell briefly. So that I may be better understood, I would like to turn to earlier times.

The Latin tongue and its perfections and greatness flourished most at the time of Cicero, for previously it was neither polished nor precise nor refined; but its perfection increased

slowly until at the time of Cicero it reached its summit. After
the age of Cicero it began to fall, and sank as in his time it
had risen; not many years passed before it had suffered a very
great decadence and diminution. It can be said that letters
and the study of Latin went hand in hand with the state of
the Roman Republic, since it increased until the age of
Cicero; and then after the Roman people lost their liberty in
the rule of the emperors, who did not even stop at killing and
ruining highly regarded men, the good disposition of studies
and letters perished together with the good state of the city of
Rome. Octavian, who was the least fierce of the emperors,
killed thousands of Roman citizens; Tiberius and Caligula
and Claudius and Nero left not one who had the appearance
of a man. Then followed Galba and Otho and Vitellius, who
in a few months undid one another. After these there were
no emperors of Roman blood, for the land was so devastated
by the preceding emperors that no man of worth remained.
Vespasian, who was emperor after Vitellius, was from Rieti
and so too were Titus and Domitian his sons; the emperor
Nerva was from Narni, his adopted son Trajan from Spain;
Hadrian too was Spanish, Severus from Africa, Alexander
from Asia, Probus from Hungary, Diocletian from Slavonia
and Constantine from England. Why do I bother with this?
Only to show that as the city of Rome was devastated by
perverse tyrannical emperors, so Latin studies and letters
suffered a similar destruction and diminution, so that at the
last hardly anyone could be found who knew Latin with the
least sense of style. And there came over into Italy the Goths
and the Lombards, barbarous and foreign nations who in fact
almost extinguished all understanding of letters, as appears
in the documents drawn up and circulated in those times; for
one could find no writing more prosaic or more gross and
coarse.

  When the Lombards, who had occupied Italy for 240 years,

were chased out and the Italian people thus recovered their liberty, the Tuscan cities and others began to recuperate.[3] They devoted work to studies and began to polish their coarse style somewhat. Thus little by little they regained their vigor, although they were weak and lacked real judgment for any fine style, since they paid attention mainly to vernacular rhyme. In this way until the time of Dante few knew the literate style and those few knew it rather poorly, as we said in the *Life of Dante*.

Francesco Petrarca was the first with a talent sufficient to recognize and call back to light the antique elegance of the lost and extinguished style. Admitted it was not perfect in him, yet it was he by himself who saw and opened the way to its perfection, for he rediscovered the works of Cicero,[4] savored and understood them; he adapted himself as much as he could and as much as he knew how to that most elegant and perfect eloquence. Surely he did enough just in showing the way to those who followed it after him. Having given himself to these studies and thus showing his virtue, Petrarca was much honored and favored while still young, and was called by the Pope to be secretary of his court; but Petrarca never agreed, nor did he value money. Nevertheless, so that he could lead an honorable life with leisure, he accepted benefices and became a regular cleric; he did this not so much by his own choice as constrained to it by necessity, for little or nothing remained from his father, and in marrying off his sister almost all the paternal inheritance was spent. Gherardo his brother became a Carthusian monk and persevered in that order to the end of his life.

3. The Lombard rule of Italy ended in A.D. 800 with the coming of Charlemagne.

4. Petrarca searched, discovered and copied a number of texts by Cicero, and wrote his famous letter to Cicero, *Rerum Familiarum*, XXIV, 3. See Ernest Hatch Wilkins, *Life of Petrarch* (Chicago, 1961), pp. 15–16, 51–53 and passim.

Petrarca's honors were so great that no man of his age was more highly thought of, not only beyond the mountains but also here in Italy; having gone to Rome, he was solemnly crowned poet. He wrote in one of his own epistles that he came to Rome for the Jubilee in 1350.[5] Returning from Rome, he took his way to Arezzo in order to see the place where he was born; the citizens had heard of his arrival and came out to meet him, as if a king had come to visit. The fame and honor attributed to him by every city and province and by all the people throughout Italy were so great that it seemed an incredible miracle. Not only the citizens and the farmers, but also the noble and great princes and lords, sought and honored him and made extraordinary provisions for his welcome. For with Prince Galeazzo Visconti he resided some time,[6] having been asked most graciously to deign to stay with him; similarly, he was honored by the lord of Padua; and his reputation and the respect offered him by those gentlemen was so great that there were often great disputes whether to send him along in his journey, or to send him to some place and favor him with more honors. Thus Petrarca lived honored and esteemed to the end of his life.

In his studies, Petrarca had one particular gift: he was very much suited to both prose and verse, and he wrote a good deal in each. His prose is graceful and elegant, his verse polished and finished and elevated in style. This gift for both the one and the other has been found in few if any but in him, for it seems that natural talent tends toward one or the other, and man usually gives himself over to that one which has the natural advantage. So it happens that Virgil, most

5. Epistle to Guglielmo da Pastrengo (Guillelmum Veronensem); see Wilkins, *op. cit.,* p. 93.

6. Following Wilkins, this would be in the summer of 1353, upon Petrarca's return into Italy from Provence. After eight years he moved to Padua, cf. Wilkins, *op. cit.,* pp. 129–186.

excellent in verse, wrote or is worth nothing in prose; Cicero, grand master of prose, is worth nothing in verse. We see the same in other poets and orators, that one of the two styles has been their source of excelling praise; but I remember having read none of them in both. Petrarca alone has been excellent in the one and the other style, through his singular gift; and he composed many works in prose and in verse, which there is no reason to enumerate, for they are known.

Petrarca died in Arquà, a village in the province of Padua, where he had chosen to live in his old age, retiring to a quiet and leisurely life separated from all complications. While he lived he kept up a very close friendship with Giovanni Boccaccio, who at that time was famous for the same studies as Petrarca; so it came about that with the death of Petrarca, the Florentine Muses became the property of Boccaccio, as if by hereditary succession; and in him then resided the fame of the previously discarded studies. It was also a succession in time, since when Dante died Petrarca was seventeen years old, and when Petrarca died Boccaccio was nine years younger than he. Thus go the Muses by succession.

ACCOUNT OF BOCCACCIO*

We shall not write a biography of Boccaccio at this time, not that he does not deserve all the highest praise but because I do not know the details of his birth or of his personal situation and life; and without knowing these one should not write. But his activity and his books are well enough known, and it is clear to me that he was a great genius, very studious and hardworking. It is to be marveled at that he wrote so much. He learned grammar only after his youth and for this reason never had Latin much in his power. But as to his writing in the vernacular, one sees that he was by nature most elegant and possessed an oratorical talent. Among his Latin works, the *Genealogy of the Gods* holds first place. He was much hindered by poverty and was never happy with his state: on the contrary, he continually wrote pleas and complaints about himself. A sensitive and disdainful man by nature, he consequently had many problems, for he did not get along on his own nor could be bear the presence of princes and lords.

* Bruni did not write more than this sketch.

COMPARISON OF DANTE AND PETRARCA

Letting Boccaccio be to investigate his life another time, I shall turn to Dante and Petrarca, of whom I say that if one must compare these most outstanding men whose lives we have written, then I affirm they were both most talented, famous and worthy of great commendation and praise. Yet since one may want to compare them with a detailed examination of their virtues and merits, and to see which has the greater excellence, I say that he must undertake no small debate, for they are almost equal in their claims to fame and glory. We can speak thus of the two of them:

Dante is of greater worth than Petrarca in the active and civic life, for he served laudably both at arms for his land and in the government of the Republic. This can not be said for Petrarca because he did not reside in a free city which had its own civil government, nor did he ever take up arms for his land, which itself is an act of great value and virtue. Dante in addition never abandoned his illustrious studies when exiled and poor, but wrote his fine work in many difficulties. Petrarca composed his works in a peaceful, quiet and honored life in which he had great prosperity. Agreed that tranquility is more desirable, nonetheless it is more virtuous to be able in the adversities of fortune to keep the mind on studies, particularly when one falls from favorable to cruel circumstances. And above all, in the science of philosophy and in mathematics Dante was more learned and more perfected, for he gave them great effort whereas in this matter Petrarca is not Dante's equal. It seems that for these reasons Dante should be given greater honor.

But turning the page and giving the arguments pertinent to Petrarca, one can reply to the first point of the active and civic life that Petrarca was more wise and prudent in choosing the quiet and leisurely life than in working in the Republic and in disputes and civic factions; for these often lead to one's being driven out by the wickedness of men and the ingratitude of the people, as happened to Dante. And certainly Giano della Bella his neighbor,[1] from whom the citizens of Florence had received so much kindness and whom they then drove away to die in exile, should have been a sufficient example to Dante that he ought not to work in the government of the Republic. Furthermore, one can reply in the same way concerning the active life: Petrarca was more consistent in keeping the friendship of princes, because he did not keep changing and modifying his position like Dante. And surely living a life respected and honored by all the lords and people was not without very great virtue, wisdom and integrity.

To the claim that Dante kept to his studies in the adversities of fortune, one can reply that in the happy life and in prosperity and tranquility it is no less virtuous to hold the mind on studies than in adversities, for prosperous circumstances corrupt the mind more than adversities. Gluttony, sleep and soft feathers[2] are prime enemies of studies. I grant

1. Tribune of Florence, Giano della Bella was a nobleman who supported the people, taking a strong stand in their cause against the privileges of the nobility. In the disorders following the arrest of Corso Donati, Giano della Bella lost favor and in 1294–95 left Florence.

2. Petrarca, *Rime* vii, *Epist. metr.,* II, 10–11.

that Dante was the more learned in philosophy and astrology and other mathematical sciences; one can yet say that in many other matters Petrarca was more learned than Dante, for in the knowledge of letters and in the understanding of Latin, Dante was much inferior. There are two parts to the Latin language, prose and verse: Petrarca is superior in both the one and the other, for he far excels in prose, and even in verse is more sublime and more ornate than Dante, so that Dante in all of the Latin language is not the equal of Petrarca. In the vulgar tongue, Petrarca is the equal of Dante in the writing of canzoni and in sonnets he has the advantage; yet I confess nonetheless that Dante's major work takes the lead over any work of Petrarca.

And yet, to conclude, each has his own excellence in part, and in part each is bested. That Petrarca and not Dante was decorated with the poet's crown has no importance for this comparison, since it is more estimable to deserve the crown than to receive it, particularly because the virtue is certain but the crown sometimes is granted lightly, so that it may be given to one who does not deserve it as well as to one who truly merits it.

6

Matteo Palmieri

CIVIC LIFE

DEDICATION[1]

My dearest Alexander, many times have I thought over how one might best live in this mortal flesh, and I have been unable to find any stability or constancy in any human condition whatsoever. Thus, without hoping to find any life perfect in every part on this earth, I arranged to devote as much time and labor as my feeble forces allowed to searching out the least stained, if not the perfect, mortal life. Since then mine has been a prolonged examination, and for a long time I have gone over the recollections of ancient histories and the greatness of noble and glorious deeds; finally the most nearly perfect life seemed to me to be one of some fine republic, where men hold to such a degree of virtue that they can live with dignity in their daily lives without error or danger and without being thought slothful. Moved by this opinion, I felt I ought to search out diligently with what arts and disciplines one might hold to such a course of life. Thus turning many pages of more and more books I found many precepts appropriate to administering the best civic life; and these, most

1. To Alexander degli Alessandri (1391–1460), prior of Florence in 1431 and gonfaloniere in 1441. Palmieri's *Della Vita Civile* was written between 1438 and 1439. Translated from *Prosatori Volgari del Quattrocento*, ed. Claudio Varese (Milan and Naples, 1955).

diligently written by various Greek and Latin authors, have been left for the well-being of the world.

Considering these many times over and knowing them to be most worthy and useful, I judged that no small fruit would follow in the life of whatever man might have even second-hand notice of them. Turning then to my cherished fellow citizens, I lamented to myself for I saw many desiring to live well and virtuously who, through no fault of their own but only for not knowing the Latin tongue, were deprived of innumerable precepts that would have well served their good intention.

I then examined which authors were likely to give adequate notice to the people, and found few who might serve[2] the virtuous, for a good many have been translated who in the original Latin were elegant, wise and serious. But they have been corrupted by the ignorance of vulgarizers, so that many are now laughable who in Latin were most worthy; and it would be much more ridiculous if I should try to demonstrate that Tully, Livy or Virgil or other translated authors were in no part similar to their originals. Yet they resemble each other only as a figure copied from Giotto's perfect hand by one whose hand had never touched pen or brush would resemble its model. Although it had a nose, eyes, mouth and all its members, nonetheless it would be different according to each man's own imagination—and perhaps in his copying Gabriel with his wings, you would not distinguish him from infernal Lucifer.

There are other writers who have written in the popular tongue, although few of high genius. First and worthy above all others is our poet Dante. He excels every other vernacular

2. *serve:* throughout this text, Palmieri uses the verb *"giovare"* meaning both "to be useful" and "to give pleasure." I have found it impossible to give a single consistent translation to the word, but have tried to preserve some of its duplicity.

writer in every way by so much that it is unworthy to compare him with them, for apart from the language, he is found but little behind the greatest Latin poets. In great things he always is sublime and elevated; in small things a diligent depictor of true propriety; one finds him gay, plain, jocund and serious, now copious and another time wondrously brief. And he is excellent not only in poetic virtue, but also as orator, philosopher and theologian. He can praise, comfort, console; and he abounds in such laudable qualities that it is better to be silent than to say little of them. But in his poetic veilings he is somewhat obscure, so that where there is not great genius and abundant learning, he is more likely to give delight than fruit. After him comes Petrarca, perhaps in a few ways his inferior, whose vernacular writings are as thoroughly moral and suitable as they could be. It is true, because the material is written diffusely, or rather because although spread out in the open it is then gathered in upon itself, that it is not much pleasing to anyone who has no abundant knowledge himself. Third then is Boccaccio, rather far behind the first in the number of his works, but worthily praised. Would to God that his vernacular books were not so stuffed with such lascivious and dissolute examples of love. Certainly I believe that had he aptly written moral things and precepts for living well, he would deserve not to be called Boccaccio but rather Chrysostom.[3] And in addition, his vernacular books would be greatly useful to our manners, whereas I think they have harmed many and continue to do so.

For these reasons, considering over and over our vernacular tongue and its lack of authors suitable to spread good

---

3. Chrysostom, fourth-century Church father. Palmieri plays on the names of the two Giovanni's: *Chrysostom* means "golden mouth" in Greek; *Boccaccio* can be considered as *"bocca"* ("mouth") plus the derogatory suffix *"—accio"* ("filthy") . Cf. *Decameron,* I, 6.

living among those who would wish to be worthy above others, I set myself to compose these books concerning the civic life, with which I might please the good, upright intention of well-disposed citizens. And in order that greater fruit should come of it, I decided not to feign the imagined goodness of citizens never seen on earth, who perfect in virtue and wisdom have been imagined and considered by Plato and other most noble geniuses; for they are depicted more in idea and figure than ever seen in the flesh. I composed this work thus drawn to show the tested way of virtuous citizens with whom one has lived and could live on earth. In it Agnolo Pandolfino, old and well-instructed citizen, expounds with an almost familial argument the order and the virtuous life of commonly praised citizens, by way of replying to questions put him by Franco Sacchetti and Luigi Guicciardini, two of the best youths of our city.[4]

The entire work is divided into four parts. In the first the newborn child is led diligently to the perfect age of man,[5] showing with what nourishment and which arts he might attain more excellence than the others. The two following books are written concerning honesty and contain the way in which the man of perfect age, in private and in public, should act according to every moral virtue whatsoever. Hence the first of these extensively treats temperance, fortitude and prudence, and other virtues contained in these; the other, which is the third book in order, is entirely given over to justice, which is the very finest part of mortal men, and nec-

4. Agnolo Pandolfini (1366–1446), Florentine statesman and writer, on whom see the biography in Vespasiano's *Renaissance Princes, Popes and Prelates* (New York, 1963), pp. 246–257. Franco Sacchetti, nephew of the fiction writer of the same name, was a friend of humanists and sometime diplomat (see Vespasiano, *op. cit.*, pp. 403–405). Luigi Guicciardini was ambassador from Florence, along with Pandolfo Pandolfini, to the court of King Ferdinand of Aragon at Naples.

5. In the tripartite scheme of the ages of man, the second stage, or manhood, is marked by the perfection of strength and reason.

essary above all else in the maintaining of a well-ordered
republic. Thus civic justice here is treated broadly: how in
peace and how in war one ought to govern, how the common
well-being ought to be provided for within the city by one
who sits among the magistrates and how outside the walls by
one who ministers publicly.

The last book only is written concerning the practical, and
sees to the richness, the adornment, the property and the
abundant wealth of the entire civic body. Then in the last
part, as an utmost conclusion, there is shown, not without
worthy doctrine, what is the state of souls who are in this
world intent upon public well-being and who live according
to the precepts of life written by us, and of their reward for
this in having been taken up to the heavens by God to eternal pleasure in glory among his saints.

After composing it, moved by the ancient care of those who
vigilantly weary themselves in leaving some worthy memory
of their continued studies, I decided to put all my work
under the worthily reputed name of an excellent man. Thus
I have writen these books in your name, knowing no one to
whom they would be more fitting than to you. You are born
of noble stock, offspring of an excellent father, raised up in
studies of the fine arts, adorned with good manners, modest,
liberal, proved truly praiseworthy, held dear by all and
exemplar of all good; your good habits clearly show in you
the firm intention to strive to attain true praise not only
according to the highest hope of the good, for also you will be
able to overcome much more with incredible virtue. I call
you to this, to this I comfort you, I beg that you force yourself to this, so that the glory of the perfect goodness of Ugo
your father and of your other renowned and glorious ancestors should reach its height in you, for he produced a supreme son well worthy of his virtue and of his family's glory.
I now, although desirous to offer you a more excellent gift,

can do no more than granted me by my strengths, which are hindered by innumerable details of private cares and above all by the intolerable necessities of public duties;[6] nonetheless I hope, whenever it may be, to see myself free from such enslavement and then to be able freely and with delight to weary myself in greater things than what I give you.

Now I beg that you accept these vulgar books such as they are, paying more attention to my well-disposed will than to the gift I make you. If you have leisure may you read them, for they show how dear you are to me; consider them, judge them and correct them, so that, polished by you and emended as much as can be, they may come into the hands of other men.

6. Elected to office in Florence, Palmieri was one of those followers of the Medici who brought about the return of Cosimo in 1434, after which Palmieri held a number of various offices until his death in 1475.

7

Giannozzo Manetti

THREE ILLUSTRIOUS FLORENTINE POETS[1]

Preface

Having recently composed six books about *Men of Great Age,* a long and laborious work, I thought it would be fitting to refresh my spirits by committing to Latin the individual lives of three illustrious poets. In *Men of Great Age* I assembled in summary form almost all the great deeds of all men who were long eminent among any people, whether for the integrity of their character, the excellence of their learning or the glory of their exploits, during a span of over 5,000 years since the world's origin; and from all these I made a single collection, like a bouquet of flowers gathered from every quarter. Many great lives, not only of our Latins, but also of Greeks and foreigners, which had been obscured and almost obliterated from our memory, partly by a lack of writers, partly by the negligence of the times (partly also they had been scattered hence through many and various codices), I have called back from darkness to the light. They were lying prostrate on the ground, and I raised them up again. So who in his right mind will think it inappropriate for me to describe domestic matters, or the lives of poets who are my fellow citizens?

1. Manetti's lives of·Dante, Petrarca and Boccaccio seem to have been written in the early 1440s. Translated from Angelo Solerti, *Le vite di Dante, Petrarca e Boccaccio scritte fino al secolo decimosesto* (Milan, 1904).

Someone may say that the very things I am now preparing to write have long since been written down by several very learned and eloquent men. I do not deny it. I admit that Dante's life was first published in his native language by Giovanni Boccaccio, a very erudite man, and that later the same poet's life, along with Petrarca's, was written more elegantly in the Florentine idiom by Leonardo Aretino, the most eloquent man of our time. Moreover, Filippo Villani, who was situated in time between these two very erudite men, brought together some things in a little Latin work on *Illustrious Florentines*. Wherefore, since it is well known that the same material has been treated by several not unworthy authors, I shall seem to have assumed this labor in vain unless I first say a few words about my reasons for writing.

It is evident that Dante, Petrarca and Boccaccio, those three illustrious poets of ours whose lives are sketched in this book, have enjoyed such continuous fame among all the common people that in the opinion of the multitude there almost seem to have been no other illustrious poets since the world began. I think this happened because in poetry and prose they surpassed all other writers in the vernacular, for in Latin they appear inferior not only to many ancient writers, but also to many new writers of our time. And so just as they are considered remarkable men, and greatly admired for their genius and erudition, by people who do not know letters and are ignorant of all learning, so all their writings in the vulgar tongue (in which they are deemed to have excelled) come to be little esteemed by the erudite and learned, who regard them as trifles or nothing at all. As a result they are praised mostly by the ignorant and unlearned, but none of the erudite now takes up their poems, or tales, or other writings of theirs, except maybe for the sake of a laugh or a jest. To my understanding this outcome is not at all in accord with the praises such great men deserve: they would not have

desired it while they were alive, nor would they wish it now
that they are dead, if they had any notion of our affairs. Every
accomplished man who ever lived has loved the praises of
distinguished and honored men, while neglecting the empty
commendations of others—as Naevius' Hector said, who
wished to be honored only by an honored man.[2] (Perhaps
that thought was not Hector's; I ascribe it to the distinguished poet Naevius.) But if learned men desire the praises
of the knowledgeable, not of others, it is surely to be supposed that if our poets care about human matters they make
little of all these commendations of the ignorant, unhonored
multitude, and derive small satisfaction from the excellent
praises of their vernacular biographers. Besides, Boccaccio
wrote only the life of Dante,[3] while Bruni joined the lives of
Dante and Petrarca but completely omitted the third. So
enough said about those two scholars.

I think a different response must be made to Villani, who
wrote the lives of our poets in Latin, not in the vernacular as
those remarkable men did. In *Illustrious Florentines* he col-
lected the lives of all our citizens who excelled in arms, or
knowledge, or art, or any capability, thus mingling the
praises of various princes, doctors, theologians, lawyers, poets
and painters. The result of this attempt was a meager commendation of our poets, like confining them in a corner
instead of giving a full treatment in accord with the abundance of their achievements.

Therefore I have undertaken to succor as best I can these
remarkable citizens of ours, these illustrious poets, by writing
new lives of them in Latin. Thus far their great merits
seemed to lie hidden among the common people; my main
purpose has been to bring them at last to the knowledge of

2. Quoted by Cicero, *Tusc. Disp.*, IV, xxxi, 67.
3. There is also a brief (and often erroneous) life of Petrarca in Giovanni
Boccaccio, *Opere Latine Minori*, ed. A. F. Massèra (Bari, 1928), pp. 238–244.

learned men, who have always set small value on vernacular writings such as form our poets' chief claim to fame.

LIFE OF BOCCACCIO (1313–1375)

Giovanni Boccaccio, an illustrious poet of his time, seemed to have succeeded Petrarca in poetry the way Petrarca had succeeded Dante a little earlier; for just as Petrarca was seventeen years old when Dante departed this life, so he was born nine years before Boccaccio. In this succession of outstanding poets, I think the almost simultaneous sprouting forth of their acute geniuses was a work of nature itself, lest poetry be thought to have vanished completely from mankind if it had lain in darkness any longer, since it seemed the human race had been left destitute for about a thousand years.

Giovanni was surnamed from his father, Boccaccio, a very honest merchant born at Certaldo, a town near Florence, as is perfectly evident from many places in his writings and from the epitaph which he composed for himself. His parents indulged him until he was a boy capable of learning, at which time, in the old way of our ancestors, he was given over by his father to literary studies. Under the grammarian Giovanni (father of a certain Zanobi,[4] a not undistinguished poet of the time) he was instructed at Florence until his father's passion for making money withdrew him from his course of study before he had learned very much; so that although Boccaccio was endowed with an acute genius, he was hardly allowed to get the alphabet. From the grammarian's school he was brought while a young boy to the school of arithmetic, in accordance with Florentine custom; thence, a few years afterward (he himself declares he had not

4. Zanobi da Strada, Petrarch's friend and correspondent, was crowned with laurel by the emperor Charles IV in 1353.

yet entered adolescence) he was handed over to a certain
great merchant of those times, to be taught commerce. He
asserts that in his six years' stay with that merchant he did
nothing but waste time: he shrank by nature from financial
arts of this sort, and he was felt to be more suited to literary
studies. For this reason he was thrust from the commercial
house and—at his father's command, and again against his
own will—set to studying canon law. (The same thing happened to Petrarca with civil law, as we said in his life.) To
his great dislike he wasted nearly as many years as he had in
commerce; for as he says, he made no progress in those
studies, because his mind quite disdained these pontifical
decrees and absurd treatises. Accordingly, when he seemed of
an age to be his own master he decided to abandon these
studies as well and turn to poetry before all else; which he
then did in the face of opposition from his father, a certain
renowned teacher, and some of his friends. And no one
should find it astonishing that neither respect for his father,
nor his teacher's authority, nor the entreaties of his friends
could keep him from abandoning canon law for poetry, since
he was so born for poetry that he almost seemed created by
God for this alone, and to shrink from everything else. To
make this clearer, I shall cite some sayings of his as reliable
evidence of such an aptitude.[5]

He himself, in fact—speaking in the last book of the *Genealogies* about the whole course of his studies—when he recounts that for the sake of gain he was handed over by his
father first to arithmetic, soon afterwards to commerce, and
then to law, writes that finally, when he had almost reached
maturity (these are the words he uses), he left off everything
else and gave his attention to poetry. He declares that he was

5. See *Boccaccio on Poetry*, ed. and trans. Charles G. Osgood (New York,
1956), pp. 129–133 (*Genealogy*, XV, x: "We Cultivate Most Those Studies
for Which We Have the Strongest Natural Bent").

by nature so born for poetry that before he had entered his seventh year, at a time indeed when he could not grasp poems on his own, or listen to others read them—in truth, he had scarcely learned the rudiments of letters—he composed (wondrous to say) some tales; and (more wondrous yet) before he had been able to understand poems he was nevertheless called a poet by everyone on account of his remarkable inventive aptitude. And a little later he says: "Now that I had almost reached maturity and was my own master, with no one urging me, no teacher leading the way—rather, against the opposition of my father, who condemned studies of this sort as frivolous and useless—I did not hesitate at least to approach the poets; and I am sure that if I had come in contact with these studies as a youth I should finally have emerged as one of the famous poets." It is evident that he said this to make clear to posterity that by nature he had been born for poetry.

Leaving aside the other arts, he engaged in these studies so unremittingly that although he was pleased by many things besides poems, only poetry retained his attention. To be sure, he studied mathematics for some years under one Andalone of Genoa, in all arts the most expert man of that time; and he also took pleasure in reading through the sacred books of Holy Scripture. But although he read all these things eagerly, afterwards he nevertheless gave them up and held fast to his study of the poets.

Since this way Boccaccio had devoted himself exceedingly late to becoming acquainted with the poets, in a very brief space of time he labored physically and mentally, through extensive transcription of Latin books and through a constant reading of the ancient poets, to attain more easily a sure knowledge of their mysteries. Lacking books and the means to buy them (since his patrimony amounted to very little), he made his own supply, copying by hand many

volumes not only of the ancient poets, but also of the orators
and historians—almost every ancient Latin text that could be
found. To contemplate the number of his transcriptions is to
be filled with wonder that a rather corpulent man like him
should have written out with his own hand so many volumes:
the task would be enough and more than enough for an
assiduous scribe who had done nothing else for most of his
life, not to say for a man very taken up with a knowledge of
things human and divine so as later to commit his thoughts to
writing (which, as will be evident below, was excellently
done by our poet) .

Not content with our abundance—or rather, scarcity—of
Latin books, he had a great desire to learn Greek letters, so
that through such knowledge he might bring aid as best he
could in those things which seemed lacking to the Latin
language. In this, I think, he imitated Petrarca, though
Boccaccio learned more of the foreign tongue. Petrarca
wished to learn from the monk Barlaam, a man very well
acquainted with Greek letters, in order that the reading of
Greek books might satisfy his insatiable desire to read. Likewise, Boccaccio for three years listened to the public and
private Greek readings of one Leontius Pilatus from Thessa-
lonica, the disciple of the aforesaid monk and later a man
very learned in Greek studies. When Pilatus was setting out
from Venice to go elsewhere, Boccaccio's advice induced him
to change his mind. He was called back by Boccaccio's promises to Florence, where Boccaccio from the first received him
respectfully into his own house, later had him as a long-term
guest, and saw to it that he was hired by the city to give
public Greek readings—the first man, it is said, to have done
so in our city. Not long afterwards, drawn by an increased
eagerness for Greek letters, Boccaccio at his own expense,
even though he was burdened by poverty, brought back from
Greece to Etruria and to his native land not only the books of

Homer but also several Greek codices. It was said that no one before him had carried Greek books back to Etruria. The first fruits in Greek letters of two so distinguished poets seem to have been a sort of seedbed, which then found richer earth and gradually so sprouted forth day by day that flowering in our times it has now brought forth rich fruits. To make this more evident, I shall take the present opportunity to review briefly the progress of Greek studies from the beginning.

Before the days of Petrarca, after the Latin language began gradually to lose its early vigor, for many centuries almost no one in Etruria mentioned Greek letters: the men of that time, content with their own learning, did not seek that of others. Petrarca, then, was the first of us who attempted to come in contact with foreign letters, studying under the monk Barlaam (as I said, the most learned Greek of the time) ; and if the unseasonable death of his teacher had not hindered him just as he was beginning to learn, Petrarca would doubtless (not "maybe," as he modestly says of himself) , considering the singular excellence of his genius and memory, have made great progress. In imitation of him, I think, Boccaccio studied three years with Leontius, in Greek letters the most learned man of that time. He learned something, and would have learned more (as he himself bears witness) if his teacher, inconstant in the old way of his forefathers, had persevered in his plan of teaching. Nevertheless, Boccaccio carried away so much from this period of instruction that among other things he had a good understanding of Homer's magnificent poems, the *Iliad* and *Odyssey;* and comprehending several other poets from his master's exposition, he made considerable use of them in his excellent book of *Genealogies*. Not long after the death of Boccaccio there emerged together several learned men, who ranged over the whole field of Latin in their youth and, following the recent example of Petrarca and Boccaccio, did not hesitate to attempt Greek itself. Wishing to satisfy their ardent desire to learn, with great promises they summoned a certain very learned man named Manuel from Constantinople, where he lived, to Florence. At public and private expense they retained him for some years until a considerable number of more learned men emerged from that quarter. What more shall I say about Greek studies, since I seem to have expounded their origin and progress at greater length than I thought to at first? This is that Manuel Chrysoloras, from whom many illustrious disciples proceeded.[6] They so spread the foreign tongue of the Greeks, like a new seedbed of letters, not only through Etruria but also through several more celebrated parts of Italy, that a short time afterwards, growing gradually until our age, it is seen to have sprouted wonderfully. But someone will say, to what purpose is all this about Greek letters? To what purpose?—so that credit for whatever Greek we know will be given to Boccaccio, who first, and at his own expense, brought back to Etruria a teacher and Greek books, which were far distant from us over land and sea.

Engaged unceasingly in humane studies of this sort until the end of his life, he left many literary monuments which are extant among us. His writings are twofold, for some were produced in his mother tongue, some in Latin. The vernacular works, partly in prose and partly in poetry, were evidently all written when he was a young man; but nevertheless we perceive they are composed with such charm and such verbal elegance that men devoid of Latin letters, provided they have a modicum of intelligence, are greatly taken by the charm of his language. Accordingly it happens that imbued by his charming manner of speech they often seem elegant. Boccac-

6. Manetti himself read Greek with Ambrogio Traversari, a pupil of Chrysoloras.

cio's Latin writings are also twofold, for he composed some in verse and some in prose. His *Bucolic Poem,* divided into sixteen eclogues, is an excellent work; and he also composed some verse epistles. All the rest of his works are in prose: nine books about *The Fates of Illustrious Men,* addressed to Carlo Cavalcante, a man of the equestrian order and prefect of the Kingdom of Sicily; one book *Concerning Famous Women,* to Lady Andrea Acciaioli, countess of Attavilla; and finally his splendid *Genealogies,* in fifteen books, dedicated to Hugo, the renowned king of Jerusalem and Cyprus. Everyone agrees that this holds first place among his works.

Since I have thus far treated of the beginning and progress of his studies, it remains for me to relate briefly his bodily appearance and his private ways. He is said to have been corpulent, tall, rather round-faced, with a pleasant and lively look, and so witty and affable in speech that his great urbanity was evident if he said a few words. Almost until maturity he had rather little amatory inclination. He was greatly vexed by poverty, because he saw that it obstructed the way by which he wished to succeed. He often knew from experience that satirist's maxim: "Not easily does a man raise himself up if his virtues are thwarted by slender resources."[7] Unable to drive off poverty itself, by constant daily and nightly toils he strove as best he could to remove, or at least reduce, the many impediments that poverty cast in the way of his glory. Wherefore with his own hand he copied many books, to satisfy in some part by this almost unceasing transcription of codices the great desire for reading that possessed him. The large number of works transcribed by him is witnessed by the noted library which Niccolò Niccoli, a man of great erudition, built—at his own expense, it is said—in the basilica of St. Augustine many years after Boccaccio's death.

7. Juvenal, *Sat.,* III, 164–165.

There they placed all the poets, together with the excellent Latin works published by him, as a perpetual testimony to Boccaccio's great and almost unbelievable diligence in transcribing codices. So proud was his nature that although he was vexed by the slenderness of his patrimony, he nevertheless could not bear to stay even a little while with any princes of the earth—the cause, I think, of his being never content with his circumstances and ardently deploring his status in many places in his writings.

After engaging in such a life of study he died at age sixty-two and was buried with honor at Certaldo in the basilica of St. James. His stone is marked with this epigram, which he composed himself:

Under this mass lie the ashes and bones of Giovanni;
His mind sits before God, rewarded for the toils
Of mortal life. Boccaccio was his father,
Certaldo his fatherland, fair poetry his study.

Coluccio Salutati, a very learned man, found these verses too humble in comparison with the poet's singular excellence, and added twelve of his own:

Illustrious poet, why speak in humble strain,
And quite pass by yourself? In brilliant song
You glorify the pastures. The names of mountains,
Woods and fountains, streams and pools and lakes
And seas you leave arranged with much labor.[8]
Illustrious men who suffered harsh misfortunes
You bring together, from Adam to our age.
In lofty style you celebrate famed mothers,
Inferior to no ancient. You give account
Of all the gods, from their unknown beginning,
Through fifteen books. A thousand toils have made you famous.
Of you no future ages will be silent.

---

8. In a compendium entitled *De Montibus, Silvis, Fontibus, Lacubus, Fluminibus, Stagnis seu Paludibus, et de Nominibus Maris Liber.*

COMPARISON OF DANTE, PETRARCA AND BOCCACCIO

Now that I have delineated as best I could the lives and characters of three outstanding poets, it remains for me to conclude with a brief comparison of them. And so wishing to compare in turn the excellences of these poets, I think it first necessary to say what is granted by everyone, that human life is twofold, active and contemplative. With this as my presupposition, I think it is not rash to say that Dante is to be preferred to the other two in almost all aspects of each life; for first he did not hesitate to bear arms and fight bravely for his homeland, and then for some time he conducted himself well in the governing of the Republic. These things pertain to the active life, and can by no means be said about Petrarca and Boccaccio. They completely disregarded the Republic, spending almost their whole lives privately in leisure and study—which is generally called the contemplative life. And so, since Petrarca and Boccaccio neglected all else, giving themselves to this alone, they certainly ought to have surpassed Dante: they had a longer, far quieter and more peaceful life. But this is far from being the case; for although Dante did not reach old age or have a long period of tranquility in his life—rather, he spent most of it drawn away from studies by the constant business of the Republic, and troubled by the various cares of exile—on account of the excellence of his genius he nevertheless in a short time acquired a great knowledge of things human and divine. In fact in mathematics, which science embraces numbers and dimensions and harmonics and the movements and revolutions of the stars, in moral and natural philosophy, and finally in the sacred Scriptures, which wholly comprehend all divinity, he made such progress that in knowledge of the aforesaid things he is not without cause set above them.

In the sum of his accomplishments, as we have said, Dante

certainly excels Petrarca and Boccaccio; but he is surpassed
by Petrarca in his entire knowledge of Latin letters and his
sure comprehension of ancient history, for Petrarca had a
greater and clearer conception of both things. Likewise,
Petrarca also has the advantage in Latin verse and prose: his
poems are more well turned and sublime, and his prose appears far more elegant. In their native language they are
considered almost equal, for if Dante is superior to Petrarca
in canzoni, in sonnets he is surpassed by him. For the rest, he
so excels Boccaccio in almost all things that he seems inferior
to him in a few quite unimportant things: in knowledge of
Greek letters, to be sure, which Dante lacked entirely, and in
Italian prose, of which he wrote little. These were the only
two things in which Boccaccio also excelled Petrarca, since in
all other things he was surpassed by him as by his teacher.

III.

THE AGE OF LORENZO

8

Angelo Poliziano

SURVEY OF EARLY ITALIAN POETRY[1]

Let no one scorn this Tuscan language as plain and meager: if its riches and ornaments are well and justly appraised, this language wll be judged not poor, not rough, but copious and highly polished. One can imagine nothing noble, ornate, graceful or elegant; nothing acute, refined, witty or subtle; nothing lofty, grand or sonorous; and finally, nothing ardent, spirited or stirring, of which infinite bright examples do not shine—not only in those two principal figures, Dante and Petrarca—but also in these others, whom you, my Lord, have brought back to life.[2]

In a Latin epistle Petrarca writes that the use of rhyme was held in high esteem even among the ancient Romans.[3] After being abandoned for a long time, it then began to flourish again in Sicily not many centuries before his time; and having spread through France, it finally came to Italy as if to its own home.

---

1. From the prefatory letter which Poliziano wrote (in the name of Lorenzo de' Medici) for the *Raccolta Aragonese,* a collection of early Tuscan poetry which Lorenzo made for Federico of Aragon, son of the king of Naples. (Lorenzo also included some of his own poems.) On the date of the letter (probably late 1476 or early 1477), and its attribution to Poliziano, see Ida Maïer, *Ange Politien, La Formation d'un poète-humaniste (1469–1480),* Travaux d'Humanisme et Renaissance, LXXXI (Geneva, 1966), pp. 226 ff. Translated from *Prosatori Volgari del Quattrocento,* where it is attributed to Lorenzo.

2. That is, by occasioning this collection of their works.

3. Cf. *Epistolae familiares,* I, 1.

Guittone d'Arezzo was the first of our writers who set his hand to depicting the lovely image of the new style; and the famous Bolognese, Guido Guinizelli, belonged to the same period. Both were very well versed in philosophy, weighty and serious; but the former was somewhat harsh and severe, not illumined by any light of eloquence. Guinizelli was much more lucid, sweet and elegant: our honored Dante does not hesitate to call him his own father and father of his "betters who ever used sweet and graceful rhymes of love."[4] He was certainly the first to give sweet coloring to the beautiful form of our idiom, which had been barely outlined by that rough Aretine. After them shines the elegant Florentine, Guido Cavalcanti, a very subtle logician and the most outstanding philosopher of his time. There is a resemblance between the man and his work; for just as he had a beautiful and graceful body, and was of most noble birth, so in his writings he has a certain something more beautiful, noble and rare than the others. He was extremely acute in invention, splendid, wondrous, very weighty in his thoughts, copious and elevated in arranging his material, orderly, wise and discerning—all of which virtues are adorned by a lovely, sweet and rare style, as if by precious vestments. If he had employed his talents in a wider field, he would indubitably have taken the highest honors. One canzone is more wonderful than all his other works. In it this graceful poet subtly described every quality, power and accident[5] of love; whence in his age the poem was so highly regarded that three of his contemporaries, most eminent philosophers (among them the Roman, Egidio), wrote very learned commentaries on it.[6]

---

4. *Purg.,* XXVI, 98–99.

5. In a philosophical sense.

6. The poem in question is Cavalcanti's *Donna mi prega.* Egidio Colonna is no longer credited with writing the commentary here attributed to him; the second contemporary commentator was Dino del Garbo; and it is not known whom Poliziano had in mind as a third.

Nor should Bonagiunta da Lucca and the notary, Giacomo da Lentino, be passed over in silence. Both were weighty and serious, but so deprived of every flower of charm that they ought to be happy if we receive them among this fair company of honored men. They were celebrated in the age of Guittone, as was Pier delle Vigne, who also composed some slight works not lacking gravity and learning. He is the one who, as Dante says,

> held both the keys
> Of Frederick's heart, and turned them
> Locking and unlocking so softly.[7]

After them shine those two wonderful suns who have made this language radiant: Dante, and not much behind him, Francesco Petrarca. About their praises—as Sallust says about Carthage—I consider it better to say nothing than a little.[8]

The Bolognese Onesto and the Sicilians were indeed the first; but just as they were more ancient than Dante and Petrarca, so they would have needed their file—though one can see that neither of them lacked talent or willingness. Cino da Pistoia lives up to his reputation very well. Wholly refined and a true poet of love, he was the first, in my opinion, who began utterly to avoid the antique roughness from which the divine Dante—most marvelous in all other respects—could not completely protect himself. After Dante and Petrarca there follows a long line of more recent writers, who are all far distant from that admirable pair.

---

7. *Inf.*, XIII, 58–60.
8. Cf. *Bellum Iugurthinum*, xix.

9

Marsilio Ficino

DANTE RETURNS FROM EXILE[1]

Florence, long sad but at last joyful, congratulates her Dante Alighieri, who after almost two centuries now lives again, restored to his native land and finally crowned with laurel:

"When you were in exile, my Dante, you once prophesied that a time would come when piety would overcome impiety and happily return you to your native land and crown you with Apollo's garlands in the lofty temple of John the Baptist.[2] Not in vain did your parents teach you the omen,[3] since recently your father Apollo took pity on my long weeping and your protracted exile. He commanded Mercury to possess the pious mind of the divine poet Cristoforo Landino, assume Landino's countenance, rouse you from sleep with his life-giving wand, carry you aloft to the walls of Florence and finally crown your temples with Phoebus' laurel. Today at last sees the divine fulfillment of Apollo's command, Mercury-Landino's pious work, Dante's prophecy and Florence's prayer. You have come at last, accompanied by a distin-

---

1. Published in 1481 as part of the proem to Landino's commentary on the *Commedia* [*No.* 10]. This translation is based on both the 1481 text and that published in Ficino's *Opera Omnia* (Basle, 1576: reprinted Turin, 1962), Vol. I, p. 840. Florence is figured as the speaker.

2. *Para.*, XXV, 1–12.

3. See Boccaccio, *Trattatello in Laude di Dante*, Chapters II and XVII; and Landino's biography of Dante [*No.* 10].

guished throng of poets: Minerva showed the way, Mercury was your guide. Finally, the Graces have happily welcomed your entrance; the Muses and Nymphs have embraced and kissed you.

> Have you come at last? The piety I counted on
> Has overcome the toilsome course, and I'm allowed
> To see your face, to hear and answer you?
> Numbering the days, I thought that this would be,
> And I was not misled by anxious care.[4]

How much more glorious, more blessed you are, dear son, than when I lost you! That former mortal countenance has become immortal and divine. The night of your Florence has been turned to day, and all the sorrow of your Florentines to joy. Rejoice, exult, you happy citizens: in place of one sun, two now rise wondrously for you, and not with fires but with redoubled beams. Today—do you not see it?—heaven itself takes open joy in your felicity. Lift up your eyes a moment to the heavens. Behold you now our Dante being crowned. 'Meanwhile the abode of all-powerful Olympus is laid open.'[5] The flames of the Empyrean have been better seen by no one: today they shimmer clearly for us, congratulating Dante on his crown. And what do you think this great sound is, so new and so sweet, that now fills our ears? Surely the sound of the nine spheres and their muses, a sound heard in no other age, today openly applauds Dante's coronation. Hear the sweet songs of the angels from Phoebus' sphere. Hear on the other hand the wonderful hymns of the archangels singing from Mercury's sphere. Glory on high to great Apollo! Glory to the Muses! Glory to the Graces! Peace, joy and happiness to the Florentines, rejoicing in their now twofold sun!"

4. Anchises' welcome to Aeneas, *Aeneid*, VI, 687–691.
5. *Aeneid*, X, 1.

10

CRISTOFORO LANDINO

COMMENTARY ON THE COMMEDIA

PROEM[1]

O most distinguished lords, there is no sort of learned writer to whom man does not owe his highest, innumerable and immortal thanks, especially when he considers that they have amassed all their work, learning, watchful studies and toilsome lucubrations in order not only to delight themselves and their contemporaries but also to offer no small usefulness to all men who succeed them across the centuries. Although I have many times read over an almost infinite number of those ingenious men who have left a memorial of themselves either in Greek or in Latin, I nonetheless find no one whom it is fitting to call the equal of that poet. For he, through his depth and variety of learning, his elegance and copiousness and sublimity of style, not only can show us great things concerning our life and salvation, but also he adorns them. He covers them with a marvelous veil in such a way that above and beyond an incomparable utility that comes from so much and varied learning there results as well an incredible delight of the soul and a pleasure of the senses which any man of erudite nature and refined perceptions takes from such a poem. But we shall speak of the poetic faculty shortly. Meanwhile, since I have been persuaded from my earliest youth,

1. Text translated .from the 1481 (first) edition of the *Comento* . . *sopra la Comedia di Danthe Alighieri.*

and since I am still moved by the authority of many learned men, who in various lands and tongues have always ranked poets above other writers, I have thus spent no small part of my years in acquainting myself with them. Now because I had recently interpreted and set out in Latin the allegorical sense of Virgil's *Aeneid,* I judged it not useless or unpleasant to my fellow citizens to investigate similarly the arcane and occult but entirely divine senses of the *Commedia* of the Florentine poet Dante Alighieri. And as I had explained the Latin poet in the Latin language, so I would interpret the Tuscan in Tuscan. It is an undertaking that doubtless would bring the highest of honors to any man of letters, for its magnitude, for the multiplicity of points involved, and above all for its novelty. Yet for me, undecorated with learning or eloquence, it would be most laborious, and perhaps not empty of foolhardiness. Nonetheless, burning love for this sort of muse has lightened my load, and as the familiar proverb of the sages has it—Nothing is difficult to the lover. All the same, there may perhaps be those who will judge our deliberations to have been in vain, if I have not brought to its proper end what I proposed at the beginning. Or they may think it superfluous, since many have commented upon this poem: these commentators may seem to have understood his mind better by having been his contemporaries, or nearer to his time; and, having been professed theologians, they may seem able more easily to have interpreted the profound meanings hidden in his work, for these have discussed the intimate secrets of theology, not without the stupefaction of the reader.

Our poet's two sons Francesco and Piero wrote commentaries, as did Benvenuto da Imola—all three in Latin. Jacopo of Bologna commented in the tongue of his land; Riccardo the Carmelite brother commented upon him; Andrea, who I think was Neapolitan, commented upon him, and Guiniforte

the lawyer of Bergamo did so as well. Our Giovanni Boccaccio began a commentary, but he did not take his work
beyond half of the first canticle. I recommend all of them, for
they said many things worthy of their learning and not useless to the reader. Finally, Francesco da Buti commented
upon him in the Pisan tongue, and he strove more than any
other but Boccaccio to open the allegorical meaning, although not in all places.[2]

My task is to tell of Dante's thought and intention according to a higher principle, and holding to it, to investigate his
more recondite learning, which is so great that when I turn
my mind to it there is born in me such horrendous stupefaction that I am as it were only a blind rat in such brightness.
As those who live near the falls of the Nile become deaf from
such excess of sound, so I lose all acumen and judgment, for
my wit is overcome by the material and by the invention, to
which not only an equal but also—unless across some great
interval—even a second is not to be found. But with divine
favor aiding my zealous will I have discovered here and there
some of the barely expressible vestiges of so divine a poet: for
I followed him first along the precipitous banks to the deep
abyss; drawn by his aid from there to the arduous mountain
ridge, I was led along the difficult way; finally, with his wings
I saw the end of so long a pilgrimage. I leave it to others
more learned than I to judge with what profit and utility I
have done it. I affirm only the following: I have liberated our
citizen from the barbarities of many external tongues in
which he had been corrupted by commentators. Now my task
seems to be to present him so pure and simple to you, most
distinguished lords, so that by the hands of this magistracy,

2. Francesco da Buti, one of the several fourteenth-century commentators
(*ca.* 1385). Boccaccio commented upon the first seventeen *canti* of the
Inferno, and initiated the public readings of the *Commedia* at Florence in
1373.

the highest of the Florentine Republic, he may be restored to his homeland after so long in exile, and so that he may be recognized as neither Romagnolo nor Lombard nor of any of those tongues of his commentators. For he is pure Florentine. And let it be a testimony of how far Florentine leads all other Italian tongues, that no one of talent or learning wrote in verse or prose who did not strive to use the Florentine idiom. But we shall speak of language shortly.

So then, O most illustrious lords, whichever of you in recognizing the divinity of Dante's genius in our book may scan the centuries and the earliest memories of all nations will be able to number him among the very select few. Furthermore, his stupendous amassing of knowledge is so varied, so recondite and so well concealed that whoever has understood it most has yet known only a small part of it, so that in recognizing it you will honor your country to which God granted such a gift. And your poet—first splendor of the name Florentine, the best, rare example of eloquence and learning—you will read frequently, for in imitating him you will adorn your orations with eloquence and dignity, your life and manners with prudence and uprightness, and your mind with learning and humanity.

Apology in Defense of Dante and Florence

Order requires that the Proem be continued and expanded with the biography of the poet. But a false and long-held opinion ingrained in the minds of many people constrains me to defer for a short time the discussion of his life, and to confute this belief, so that at one and the same time both my homeland and the poet may be freed from the grave calumny which has unworthily insulted both the one and the other. In various parts of the *Commedia* people read bitter invectives against the Florentines who were ruling in those days and harsh criticisms of their various vile doings. This seems not

only to be a disgrace to the city but also to carry some reproach to the poet, thus obscuring the fame of his homeland
which, like a dutiful and pious son, he ought to have praised.
First then we shall demonstrate that Dante did not disgrace
the homeland. Then, by discussing several examples of the
governmental administration, we shall prove both that our
Republic should not be criticized and, to the opposite and
necessary point, that those without envy who do not lack
judgment hold our Republic among the most highly distinguished. Yet this will be only the beginning. Our poet was of
so generous a mind that he would have disdained to make
himself openly a Florentine had he judged it an infamous
land. Thus he judges Florence a most noble city. But it is not
necessary to search out conjectures of his opinion and of what
he felt concerning his homeland, for in many places he
praises it thoroughly. For example, in the *Inferno* he calls it
noble homeland through the mouth of the magnanimous
Farinata; and in Canto XXV of the *Paradiso* he desires above
all else to return there to what he calls the fold,[3] the sheepfold and shelter of kindly and benign souls; and this praises
the city and praises the people it contains both for beauty
and for virtue. And in the fifteenth canto of the *Paradiso* he
says, "Florence within the ancient circle from which it takes
tierce and nones remained in sober and modest peace."[4]
What greater praise can there be of a Republic than living in
peace? For this cannot come about without the greatest
prudence and justice; and living "sober and modest" repre-
sents the two virtues which make up perfect temperance. But
I ask you, let us read this whole canto and we shall understand how miraculously the good poet praises his ancient
homeland, especially in these verses: "To so quiet and beau-

3. *Para.*, XXV, 1 ff.
4. *Para.*, XV, 97–99: "Fiorenza dentro dalla cerchia antica/ ond'ella toglie
ancora e terza e nona,/ si stava in pace, sobria e pudica."

tiful a life of citizens, to so faithful a populace, to such a pleasant abode."[5] And in the sixteenth he writes: "With these people and with others as well I saw Florence in such repose that there was no reason to mourn. With these men I saw your people so glorious and just that the lily was never dragged in defeat nor turned crimson in division."[6] What slander can be spread or rather praise be taken from a just people? They cannot be other than supremely continent, and also glorious, for glory cannot derive otherwise than from many excellent and enduring virtues. I leave aside many other places in which he exalts and extolls so great a city with every sort of praise. But someone may perhaps say, "Read the places where he disgraces the Florentines." To which I reply that he does not disgrace the Florentines, whom he calls sober and tranquil, glorious and just, as we have shown. But he disgraces those Florentines who by their ambition and factionalism had become unjust, rapacious, cruel and avaricious. Just as Sallust[7] did not disgrace Rome in slandering the ambition, the luxury and the avarice of his times, and in addition the perfidy of Catiline and Lentulus and the other conspirators; nor was there disgrace in his observing the enormous infamy of Albinus or Calfurnius or Scaurus or many others. But in praising the ancient Roman discipline he shows how much these had degenerated from their ancestors. Dante shames the atrocious governors, or rather the thieves of his people: it is they whom he affirms, in that well-known passage, to be the wolves in the sheepfold of San

5. *Para.*, XV, 130–132: "A così riposato, a così bello/ viver di cittadini, a così fida/ cittadinanza, a così dolce ostello."

6. *Para.*, XVI, 148–154: "Con queste genti e con altre con esse,/ vid'io Fiorenza in sì fatta riposo,/ che non avea cagione onde piangesse:/ con queste genti vid'io glorïoso/ e giusto il popol suo, tanto che 'l giglio/ non era ad asta mai posto a ritroso,/ nè per divisïon fatto vermiglio." Landino's text here reads "popol *tuo*," which I follow in the translation.

7. See Sallust, *Bellum Catilinae,* xviii and passim.

Giovanni. And this we must grant him, whether because he narrated the truth or if because with tragic invective against the worst citizens, that is against the impious tyrants, he darts his satirical verses like a new Archilochus[8] in the form of poisonous arrows. Nevertheless, although he may do this in some places, in most places he honorifically exalts and adorns with perpetual fame many other people who are worthy of true praise. I add again that having been unjustly exiled and made an unfaithful rebel from those of his homeland, he deserves excuse if sometimes in his righteous disdain he exceeds the norm. And this is enough in defense of the poet. . . .

[There follows a lengthy defense of Florence and the Florentines.]

. . . I notice that by drawing out my material in diverse directions I am becoming too wordy and I find myself moving away from the end. But in the midst of telling so many virtues of my people, there may perhaps be one who will want to reproach them for ingratitude at having unjustly put into exile a citizen who was so useful and so graced with every virtue; and then they never called him back. To which the reply is easy: this was a fault of the times, and not one of the nature of the people. And if we search out the truth, we shall see that it was the power of the few in whose opinions rested the entire public administration that committed such an atrocity, and not without the greatest sadness among the people. From this I derive a conjecture: since the people were unable during Dante's lifetime to use their liberty, why did they not use it after his death, when the leaders of the adverse faction were already fewer and to some extent less

---

8. Greek lyric poet, *ca.* 680–640 B.C. Frederic Will, in his *Archilochus* (New York, 1969), observes that the Greek poet was attacked by various Christian writers for his notable freedom of spirit. Will (pp. 79–80) cites Clement of Alexandria and Eusebius.

threatening? They might by public decree have entrusted to the prefects of the construction of the Duomo that at that time in an honorable place they should at public expense build to our poet a sculptured marble tomb with those statues and symbols which would make it most beautiful to see.[9] But even this was prevented by the envy of the few in power.

You then, most illustrious lords, for the force of such a decree which for some time now has been abrogated and derogated, and for the prayers of the Florentine people who desire it above all, and for your pity toward the father of your country, may he be given back to his city and find a place in that temple which is the great cathedral, and may there be established there an appropriate and honorable seat for him; thus may he at last rest where before his exile he worked long hours for the preservation of your liberty. Surely if the Athenians deemed it so honorable to be harbored for one's merit, at public expense, in the Pyrtaneum, their curia, then the piety of the Florentines and the merits of the poet request in the utmost that there should be a monument to him, not only in public but in a sacred and majestic place. Divine precepts will wish it. Human laws demand it. Every sort of natural justice desires it. And it is very much to the point of public utility that the prizes and honors of the dead should spark the living to imitate the traces of those who by their immortal virtue have changed from mortals to immortals. Who is there who does not know that the brightest of flames is the fame and glory of those who live forever although already dead? It always incites the human breast to every eminent virtue and understanding. That city can never be vile in which various rewards are always placed in front of

9. It was decreed in 1396 that Dante's bones should be brought to Florence and a suitable tomb constructed in the Duomo. The text is printed in *Il Processo di Dante,* ed. Dante Ricci (Florence, 1967).

learned men; for the wise remark of Plato is true and entirely sybilline, that those republics will always do well in which the philosophers govern or else in which the governors begin to philosophize.[10] But because I know it is superfluous to spark him who burns or to urge on the one who is running fast by himself, I will not cogitate nor longer orate in persuading you, our most noble lords, of that to which your kindly nature always inclines you. For this reason, leaving behind every exhortation, I shall come with only the briefest of words to the poet's life, which I cannot pass over completely, if I do not wish thus to omit the well-established and always observed practice of every interpreter of poetry. Nor ought I to relate it at great length, for by many other learned men, and above all by Gianozzo Manetti, it has been fully and elegantly told.

Life and Customs of the Poet

It is better and better known from many noble writers of no small authority that Eliseo was born of the noble family of the Frangipani; the family was of senatorial rank in Rome and of them was born also Saint Ambrose. Eliseo, after our city was recovered from Charlemagne, came to Florence and took residence in Sesto San Piero near the Donati and the Pazzi. From him the successors, having abandoned the name of Frangipani, were called Elisei and flourished for a long time in the Republic. Among these was Cacciaguida, who married a maid from Ferrara of the noble family of the Aldighieri, and thus one of her children was named Aldighieri. Because he was held in highest authority and veneration in the Republic for his excellent virtues, he, as Eliseo had changed the name of the Frangipani, so changed the

10. Plato describes the philosopher-king particularly in the *Republic*, V, 473, c and following.

name of the Elisei and from his time they were called Aldighieri. Then having removed the letter *d* they called themselves not Aldighieri but Alighieri. Others say that they did not take the family name from this man, but from the wings [*ale*] which it is clear they had as their family device. But I leave this to be investigated by the more curious.

I assert only that there was born another of the same name from the descendants of the first Alighiero, and he fathered Dante, our poet, in the year of our Lord MCCLX, during the pontificate of Clement the Fourth. Nor can I omit mention of a marvelous dream that appeared to his mother shortly before the child's birth. She seemed to be in a green and flowering field, near a crystal fountain and under a high laurel, where she gave birth to a son who for a time nourished himself on the laurel berries and the water of the nearby fountain. And having grown up in a short space of time, he became a shepherd; wishing to take some branches of the laurel, he fell, but quickly rose up no longer a man but changed into a peacock. This denoted what Dante would be. Such a dream was interpreted at length by Boccaccio.[11] But I, in short, believe that by the shepherd is understood his philosophical and theological learning, on which every well-disposed mind may excellently feed itself; and the highly decorated feathers of the peacock foretell his elaborate poem. No one need marvel at this, for often and in various places and centuries there have occurred strange events which predicted the excellence of some man. For one reads of Virgil that the night before his birth his mother dreamed she bore a laurel branch, which in a short time became a great tree and was filled with various fruits and flowers. Astyages, king of the Medes, dreamed that from the genitals of his daughter

11. *Trattatello in Laude di Dante,* pp. 572–573, in the edition by Pier Giorgio Ricci of Boccaccio's *Opere in versi* (Milan and Naples, 1965).

was born a grapevine, the shoots of which in a short time shadowed over all Asia: the interpreters of the dreams responded that from her would be born a very powerful man who would oppress his country.[12] Nor did it occur otherwise, since the daughter gave birth to Cyrus, who occupied Persia and transferred the kingdom of the Medes to the Persians. Not only dreams but also other miraculous occurrences foretell the same. For one reads that the bees brought honey to the mouth of Plato, when still very young he lay in his cradle; this predicted the future sweetness of his eloquence and learning.

But I return to the poet. From his earliest years, Dante was of the finest disposition and showed evident signs of his future integrity and genius; already in his childhood one could see in his face the figure of an acute man, and all his manners were dignified. It was a small indication of his generous and gentle spirit, full of humanity, that he was ardently taken with love for the daughter of Folco Portinari, a young girl called Bice, whom Dante henceforth always called with the more worthy name Beatrice. As he shows in his verses, she was then in her eighth year, and he not out of his ninth. This became so impressed on his brain that he not only loved her as long as she lived, but then after her death in her twenty-fourth year he mourned her bitterly for a long time. This love of corporeal beauty, although it may be degenerated from true divine love and that furor described by Plato, is nothing less than an effigy and image here on earth of that other love; so long as it be chaste and modest, it deserves not blame but praise. For by those earthly beauties we raise ourselves to the divine. Furthermore it may happen to one who has poetic genius that the sweet bitterness of love often awakes and excites him to the writing of amatory poems and sharpens his talent and gives him eloquence.

12. Cf. Herodotus, I, 108.

How ardent were his studies in every discipline is beyond belief; and in his earlier years he took great profit from the oratorical faculty, even more than from the poetic. In these arts his preceptor was Brunetto Latini, a man greatly learned insofar as the coarseness of those times allowed. Next he practiced dialectic and all mathematics; he exercised himself in moral and natural philosophy, and he took great delight in music—he was familiar with all the musicians of his time who had any reputation at all. Nor did his spirit lack the strength of military training, for often he found himself involved in war; and in the most perilous battle of Campaldino, as he writes in his letter, he brought forth honor to himself and to his land by fighting manfully.

But I return to his love, concerning which we can point to these verses of Horace:[13]

> Place me, where desert wastes forbid
> One tree to breathe the summer wind,
> Where fogs the land and sea have hid,
>   With Jove unkind;
> Or, where the sun so near would be,
> That none to build or dwell may dare;
> Thy voice, thy smile, my Lalagè,
>   I'll love them there.

So grievous was his longing for the dead Beatrice that he lived in constant sadness and tears. Although they tried very hard, his friends found no sort of consolation with which they might in the least mitigate so much misery. Long duration of time did not help, and he took no pleasure in different activities nor in prosperous or opposite things. Thus it was that his friends suggested they should get him married, hoping

13. *Odes*, I, xxii, 17–24 (trans. W. E. Gladstone). The poet-lover, Horace had suggested with mock solemnity, has no need for weapons; for as he wandered through the woods unarmed, singing of Lalage, a wolf had fled from him.

that the new and living love of his lawful wife might extinguish the old flame. After all, it is the wisdom of the philosophers, which he himself repeated, that just as one draws a nail from a plank with another nail, so from the human breast one may draw out the old love with a new love. The elegiac poet expressed it thus: *Successore novo tollitur omnis amans.*[14] But the faithful advice led to an opposite end. He married one who was surely very noble, born from the ancient family of the Donati and called Gemma; and she was worthy of praise for her other manners, but so peevish and aloof that she took the prize from Socrates' Xanthippe. This caused the appearance of contrary habits, which by their greater force took up again the love of Beatrice: as this love had inspired and refined him in many liberal arts, so Gemma was an annoying impediment to him in many things. And finally, although she would have borne him more children, he was constrained to separate her from himself. He did not, either in his homeland or in exile, live with her again.

He showed no less genius and wise counsel in civil government and administration than in learning; and so much did he love justice and public tranquility that in the pestilential civic dissension of those times he, although a Guelf and a supporter of the Church, all the same tried constantly with all his effort to bring about public agreement. For these virtues he was so loved by the people that he won every office in the selection of magistrates, who were then chosen not by lot but by public vote. Rising through each rank, he was created a prior, the highest magistrate of our Republic, in his thirty-fifth year. But often those things which are subjected to the temerity of fortune bring with them this adversity: whence we hope for great peace is born great and disturbing travail.

---

14. Ovid, *Remedia Amoris,* 462. The text as recent editors have it reads "omnis *amor.*" "Every love is conquered by a succeeding new love."

This was Dante's experience. The magistracy, from which he hoped to have the most ample recompense for his having administered with the greatest calm, was the cause of his exile because the city was already diseased with the Whites and the Blacks, of whom we shall talk extensively in the first cantica, for these were the two parts into which the Florentine Guelfs were divided. In vain our poet tried with all his effort to bring about concord among his citizens and to end the disagreements by showing that they would weaken the forces of the Guelfs so much that they would give certain victory to the Ghibellines. And finally, unable to make improvements, he decided to leave public administration and to live with leisure among letters; but the pleadings of his friends—and perhaps some ambition on his part—won out over the contrary proposal.

The discord was increasing every day, along with such recklessness among the Black princes that they, seeing the Whites prevailing, met in the Church of Santa Trinita and after long consultation decided to send to Pope Boniface and ask that he send someone of royal stock and authority to reconcile our Republic and to quell the disorders. It vexed Dante that public councils should be held in a private place by private citizens without the decree of the highest magistrate. For this reason he persuaded those who were his fellow governors that such authority should be repressed and the leaders punished. His own authority had such effect that messers Corso Donati, Geri Spina, Giachinozzo de' Pazzi, Rossa della Tosa, and several other Black princes were exiled. And finally messer Gentile and messer Torrigiano de' Cerchi, messers Guido Cavalcanti, Baschieri della Tosa and Baldinaccio Adimari were pronounced exiles from the White party. Shortly thereafter, since the discord did not cease, he was created emissary to Boniface. In this mission he was full of doubts, because it seemed to him that in going away he would leave the city in danger, and he did not see anyone to whom he might easily delegate such a mission. Thus abstracted in deliberation he was heard to say, without thinking himself heard: "If I go, who will stay? And if I stay, who will go?" His rivals ascribed these words to great arrogance, as if he judged the public government to reside only in him. Finally he went. And after he left, messer Corso Donati returned and with his faction had such success that Dante and many other noble citizens were exiled and their possessions confiscated.

This was the reward our poet won for his many great efforts to lead his people to peace and concord. For this reason, since he had in vain tried many times to placate his enemies, he joined with the Florentine exiles; they elected Alexander count of Romena as their captain and tried to return by means of force. But this did not succeed; he crossed the Apennines and was kindly received by Alberto della Scala, lord of Verona. He turned to prayers and humble pleas, and wrote from there many times to Florence; and both in public and in private he asked for nothing but to be called back. Not succeeding, he finally went to Paris; there, although he suffered much from poverty, he turned all his study to philosophy and theology. It was marvelous that among so many learned men, he was inferior to no one in disputation; and he was restored entirely into the graces of the Muses.

When the emperor Henry passed into Italy, new hope of returning was kindled in Dante. He returned to Italy and persuaded the emperor, who threatened the Florentines because they had not been willing to promise a reception of his emissaries in the city, that he should leave his enterprise in Brescia, which he had besieged, and occupy Florence. Henry came through Liguria to Pisa, and from Pisa went by sea to Rome. From there, having conquered his adversaries, he took the crown. Angered against Robert king of Sicily and against the Florentines, he came to Florence. But again the way failed, because Henry came in vain and in vain camped at Santo Salvi, a mile distant from the city. After a few days, having lost all hope, he took the road to Rome and at Buonconvento, a Sienese castle, he became ill and died.

Dante passed into the Romagna and was kindly received by Guido Novello, lord of Ravenna, and he took residence there. After several years he spent the last day of his life in his sixty-sixth year, and he was buried with no ordinary exequies in the church of the Minorites.

He was of medium and suitable height, had a rather long face and somewhat large eyes, an aquiline nose, and large and angular jaws. His lower lip was proportionately larger than his upper. His coloring was brown, his beard and hair black and curly. Hence the joke was told in Ravenna that when Dante passed by some women, one of them said, "He has been to Hell and returned," to which the one beside her replied, "I believe it, for he turned black from the darkness and smoke and his hair was darkened by the fire."

His effigy done by the hand of Giotto his contemporary rests in Santa Croce and in the chapel of the Podestà.[15] He always dressed modestly even before his exile when he still had an ample patrimony. He was serious but gracious in appearance and speech. In eating and drinking he was very continent, for which reason he always hated the voracious and gluttonous. His thoughts were fixed and profound, and he had so much desire to read new things that he carried a book with him in unlikely circumstances; where people were dancing in solemn celebration in great numbers, he would read unstintingly, fixing his thoughts so much upon the book that in reading it he neither saw nor heard anything else. In

15. I.e., the Bargello.

extemporaneous oration he was very eloquent, and for this reason he obtained a most honored place in the Republic for many years, and was sent by his land as emissary to many princes and republics.

All men agree that Dante first brought back to the light the ornaments of poetry and rhetoric; and the elegance, temperance and dignity of the ancients, which had been extinguished for many years, he brought back to the light in great part. In Latin he wrote eclogues, which show poetic genius, and they involve so much knowledge of antiquity that one ought not to desire more from those coarse times. In the same language but in prose he wrote three books entitled the *Monarchy.* Likewise the *De vulgari eloquentia.* In Florentine prose he wrote the *Convivio* and the *Vita Nuova.* In verse he wrote many sonnets and canzoni in which it is marvelous that to the material of love, in which he disclosed all his sentiments, he added very subtle allegories of deepest philosophy and theology in which there appears stupendous learning. He wrote the *Commedia,* which we have interpreted, and divided it into three canticles. He began it before he was sent into exile. But the final canti of the *Paradiso* remained hidden in a secret part of the house he was living in at the time of his death. With great vexation every man who read the poem desired them; but the ghost of the poet appeared at night in white clothes to his son Jacopo and showed him where they were.[16] The young man awoke, immediately looked for them and found them.

We shall endeavor shortly to show the divine virtues of that work. In the meantime, we shall give innumerable and utmost thanks, for he was the first who ennobled with fullness and elegance, with erudition and ornament our own

---

16. Umberto Cosmo, in his *Guida a Dante* (trans. David Moore, *A Handbook to Dante Studies* [Oxford, 1950], p. 142) observes that the story is "a fact which, when stripped of all irrelevancies, cannot be doubted."

native tongue, which until his times was coarse and unused. Homer found the Greek tongue already more abundant and cultivated by Orpheus and the Muses, and by other poets older than he. Virgil found Latin already polished and ornamented, and enlarged by Ennius and Lucretius, by Plautus and Terence. But before Dante, in the Tuscan language no one had found any grace or brought in any elegance or light; and except for rhymes, although even they were still inept and coarse, the ancients have nothing in which one sees the least vestige of a poet. Dante was the first to have learned among the Latin writers the ornaments which are common to the orator and the poet and to have understood how much acute genius is necessary to poetic invention. And so too how much judgment in disposition, how many different colors and lights in elocution, and moreover with how many fictions the poem must be veiled and of how much and how varied learning it must be reckoned—Dante was the first who tried with happy auspices to bring all these to our tongue. In the centuries past no one had tried it. For this reason he gave it an origin, he led it far toward perfection, which has happened few times among mortals. He first showed how suitable was the Florentine tongue not only to express but also to fill out and decorate all that which falls into discussion.

Francesco Petrarca succeeded Dante. What an immortal man, Lord, and worthy of what admiration! I do not doubt that in his songs and sonnets he not only equals the first lyric and elegiac Greek and Latin poets, but surpasses many. And in lyric verses Pindar is by common consent supreme, whom Horace worthily affirms to be inimitable;[17] and in Greece there were those who contended that he surpassed Homer. Surely for magnificence of spirit, for sense and for figures he excels all others; and there was no one who better succeeded

17. Cf. Horace, *Odes*, IV, ii, 1 ff.

at forming words combined from others. But this is so much part of the Greek language, that neither Latin nor Tuscan can do it. But by God, let it be said without envy: consider how often Petrarca rises and lifts himself up like a swan; consider how full of wise judgments he is, and how many of these are contained in every part. He is harsh in his invective and criticism, and he pursues vices with that vehemence with which Alcaeus struck the tyrants in his verses. In the sentiments of love he is now gay, now sad, and he expresses all of them graciously, which I would propose of neither Ovid nor Propertius. But above all he takes the palm in the fact that in every frivolous matter, even though it be most playful, he nonetheless observes a happy modesty and never becomes obscene. None of the most eloquent people will deny that they find in him not only expressed but also vividly depicted many things which they had before judged impossible to say with any eloquence in this language.

Then followed Boccaccio, very inferior to him, although he was a poetic genius taught by nature, and very ornate in invention. Bonifacio Uberti[18] could be numbered among the poets if in him nature and practice were aided by art and learning. Baptista Alberti[19] has expanded our language very much, and in loose oration and prose has surpassed and defeated all his superiors; and his eclogues written in Tuscan verses show how learned he is in poetics and with how much judgment he abounds.

But already there is flourishing he who—if my judgment is worth anything—will be in the first of the most rare.[20] Surely

18. Fazio degli Uberti (*ca.* 1305–1367), author of the *Dittamondo*, a historical poem in *terza rima*, and of some lyrics.

19. Leon Battista Alberti (1404–1472), perhaps the best example of the all-round man of the Renaissance, wrote philosophical prose, treatises on art and architecture, and poetry, and showed his talent and learning both in Italian and in Latin.

20. Lorenzo de' Medici, Landino's pupil.

his genius is marvelous and it is so *eutrapele,* as the Greeks say, that is, suitable to everything, that wherever he turns it seems that he was born solely to that. Doubtless every sort of poetry comes to him by divine influence. He is most wise in invention and supremely rich in elocution, so that he gives majesty to great things and dignity to the mediocre. In sum, so great is his style that although it may appear vulgar to commoners, it can only be imitated with difficulty by the learned. For in him art competes with nature, and each excellently defends its share. Surely he would be a marvel even among those who have consumed much time in literary leisure and in studies. What then shall we say of him, who in his youthful years was capable of so much, particularly in his so many and varied and great occupations in public government, which not without great dangers distracted him day and night, since he could not for a moment leave them? I do not deny how much natural genius can do in this case; nonetheless, if from his tender years he had not given himself with most ardent study to Latin letters and to oratory and if to my most faithful precepts he had not with great industry been obedient, no one thinks that the strength of his nature alone would have raised him to so high a level. My tongue cannot express what my mind feels about him; but whoever will read what he has written will know me to be more stingy in commendation than prodigious in adulation.

But in turning back to our language, I assert that as in the older centuries first the Greek language and then the Latin, through a great many writers who polished it across the years, turned from poor and coarse to finely finished, so too with our tongue. Already now by virtue of the writers whom I have mentioned it has become abundant and elegant, and every day, if studies are not lacking, it will improve all the more. But let there be no one who thinks himself not only an eloquent but even a tolerable writer, if he have not first a true and perfect understanding of Latin letters. For no one doubts that all discourse is composed of words and thoughts: the words are always inept without the oratorical precepts and the thoughts are frivolous without varied learning. But neither theoretical art, nor any other doctrine, can be known without either Greek or Latin language; thus the Latin at least is necessary. This fact has brought it about that many of our writers who lack Latin letters and learning, although their genius and labor sometimes sustains them, nonetheless often they come to ruin; for they proceed like blind men, if the light of art is not carried. Nor can the writer have blood or nerves to his style when he is not at least trained in philosophy, even if not completely learned. Add to these two reasons the third: everyone understands how the Latin tongue became abundant by deriving many words from the Greek; thus it is necessary that ours will become even richer than it is if every day we transfer into it more new words taken from the Romans and make them commonplace among our own. For this reason, let the Florentine youth exercise itself in the studies of the arts and in its native tongue, and let that make it yet more eloquent. Nothing is found that in a free and well-founded republic brings more utility and honor than true eloquence, whether of oratory or of poetry; it is accompanied by true virtue and the highest integrity. It can bring the hatred of the good citizens to bear upon the villainy of the bad and lead them to torment; it can free the innocence of the impotent from the punishment of false judgments; it can urge the people, who are slow of themselves, toward those things in which the public honor resides, or it can call them back from error or inflame them against harmful citizens or calm them when they have been roused against the good citizens. In Athens Demosthenes and in Rome Cicero, although both were of the lowest condition, eloquence raised up and made superior in dignity to all the most noble citizens. Our poet, who was already cultivated in all learning, recognized this and judged the ability to adorn every grave thought with eloquence to be of surpassing excellence; for having practiced long in prose and in verse, he became so eloquent that finally, honored with wisdom and eloquence, he began to write the *Commedia* which we now have in our hands. Of its magnificence and adornment we shall speak in the appropriate place.

11

Ugolino Verino

"EULOGY OF THE POET FILELFO, WHO DIED IN FLORENCE AT AGE NINETY"[1]

If fair Apollo mourned the poet Homer,
    and Calliope bewailed the death of Linus,
now you, Ausonian Nymphs and Greek Camenae,
    honor the learned old man's obsequies.
Sing the surpassing praise of your Filelfo,   5
    who acquainted the Latin Muse with Grecian measures.
Many Greek monuments he brought to us,
    and many by his labor he made known.[2]
He explicated Dante and acutely
    made clear the varied odes of terse Petrarca.   10
He sang Francesco Sforza's conquering arms,[3]
    a poem that rivals Homer's lofty style.
Here to our country he brought Chrysoloras,[4]
    whence Grecian nectar reached Ausonian lips
and now Italians, fluent in Greek speech,   15
    adorn Oenotria with foreign flowers.

---

1. Exiled by Cosimo in 1434, Filelfo had been recalled by Lorenzo in 1481 and died that same year (at the age of eighty-three). Translated from *Poeti Latini del Quattrocento,* F. Arnaldi, *et al.* (Milan and Naples, 1964).

2. Filelfo brought back many codices from his stay in Constantinople (1421–27), and was an accomplished translator from Greek.

3. The *Sforziad* was begun in 1451.

4. Something of an exaggeration, since Filelfo was born a year after Manuel Chrysoloras began teaching Greek in Florence. At Constantinople Filelfo studied with Manuel's brother John, whose daughter he married and did bring back to Italy.

Now was desired the old man's eloquence,
  and he about to explain the Socratic books—
Cruel Fates! whom neither reverence for white hair
  nor Medicean piety could turn back.   20
Behold, in his old age return was granted
  by the grandson of that man who exiled him.
Better this than dying in Milan: he saw,
  after three generations, his fatherland.[5]
And Florence was not harsh, as once to Dante,   25
  spitting out an honored old man's bones:
the senate made magnanimous provision
  to keep the bard from dying far away,
established a stipend for the learned bard,
  mindful of us and mindful of itself.   30
But since cruel Fate spares no one and one day
  bears all away, farewell, learned Filelfo.
You will go to heavenly groves, the lovely places
  of pious souls, amidst bards crowned with laurel:
before you Claudian, dweller by the Nile,   35
  but ours by birth, who sang a general's deeds;
to your right, Dante; to your left, Petrarca;
  and your path followed by Boccaccio.
In such a triumph, with such retinue,
  you will go, learned Filelfo, to the heavens.   40

5. During his earlier stay in Florence, Filelfo had been granted honorary
citizenship.

12

Lorenzo de' Medici

JUSTIFICATION OF THE
COMMENTARY ON HIS SONNETS[1]

I have had some doubts whether to do the present interpretation and commentary on my sonnets. If I was sometimes
inclined to do it, the following contrary reasons came and
took me away from this work. First, I seemed likely to incur
some presumption in commenting on my own works, both by
the excess of self-esteem I would show and in seeming to
assume that judgment which ought to be made by others, and
in this latter point I would seem to observe that the intelligence of those into whose hands my verses will go might be
hardly sufficient to interpret them. In addition I thought as
well that someone of little judgment might easily criticize my
having used my time to write and comment on poems the
matter and subject of which were an amorous passion; and
this would be more reprehensible in me for my continued
tasks, both public and private, which ought to have drawn
me away from similar thoughts, which some people think not
only frivolous and of little matter but also pernicious and of
some harm to our soul as to the honor of the world as well. If
this is so, then thinking such thoughts is a great error, putting them into poetry is much greater, but commenting upon
them seems no less a fault than to make a lasting and set habit

---

1. Translated from Emilio Bigi, *Scritti scelti di Lorenzo de' Medici* (Turin,
1965).

of evil works. All the more because commentaries are reserved for matters of theology and philosophy and great
effects that involve either the edification and consolation of
our minds or the practical matters of human life. Furthermore, one may add this, that it will perhaps seem reprehensible to some people that I have written and spoken of
worthy matters and subjects in our maternal vernacular
tongue, for where it is spoken and understood by being very
common it seems to tend to a certain low worth, and in those
places where it is not known it cannot be understood, and
there in those parts our work and task seem entirely vain and
in effect are the same as if they had never been done.

Until recently these three difficulties have held back the
present interpretation, which I had proposed quite some
time ago. Convinced in my opinion and by better reasons,
however, I have now considered putting it out, thinking that
if my small task will be esteemed and found pleasant by
someone, it will then find its place and not be wholly vain.
And yet if it be ill received, it will be read little and exe-
crated by few, and in its not being very long-lasting the
criticism it may undergo will not endure for long.

And, in now replying to the first criticism and to those who
would like to consider me presumptuous in any way, I say
that it does not seem to me presumption that I should interpret my own things, but rather a lightening of the task of
others.[2] And the office of interpreter is more proper to no
one beyond the writer himself, for no one can better know or
select the truth of his meaning, as is shown clearly enough in
the confusion arising from the varieties of commentaries in
which most frequently the personal nature of the writer is
followed rather than his real intention. Nor does it seem to
me that in this argument I should take too much account of

2. Cf. Dante, *Convivio,* I, ii, 1 ff.

myself or take the rights of judging away from others, because I believe that the true office of every man is to do everything to the benefit of mankind, whether himself or others. And because not everyone is born ready to do those things which are held best in the world, every man ought to measure himself and see in what activity he can best serve the human race, and he should exercise himself in that. For one thing alone cannot satisfy both the diversity of human minds and the necessity of our life, even if it is the best and most excellent work men can accomplish. On the contrary, it seems that contemplation, which is incontrovertibly the best and most excellent [*lacuna*]; and thus one concludes that not only many works of genius but also many wicked offices combine by necessity in the perfection of human life, and that it is the true duty of all men to serve the human race in that degree to which they find themselves disposed, whether by heaven or nature or fortune. I would have liked very much to exercise myself in greater things; but I do not for this want to let down any one person,[3] if not many, who perhaps rather to please me than because my works satisfy them have encouraged me in this task. Their authority and kindness are worth much to me. And if I cannot otherwise be useful to my readers, at least they will be able to take some bit of pleasure from my poems, because they may perhaps find some genius proportionate and in accordance with their own. Yet if someone should laugh at them I will be grateful that he takes pleasure from my verses, even if it is slight; for it seems to me above all that in publishing this interpretation I submit myself to the judgment of others. If I had judged myself that these verses are unworthy of being read, I would have avoided the judgment of others; but in commenting upon them and publishing them, in my opinion, I much better avoid the presumption of my judging myself.

3. Possibly Pico della Mirandola, who called the *Commentary* "mea paraphrasis" in the letter of July 15, 1484.

Now to reply to the calumnies of those who would like to accuse me of having spent time both in the composing and in the commenting of things unworthy of any time or effort, since they are amorous passions, etc., and particularly in the midst of my many necessary duties, I say that in fact I would be condemned justly, when human nature would be endowed with such excellence that all men might always do everything perfectly. But since this degree of perfection is granted to very few and to these few only rarely in their lives, it seems to me that I may conclude, with all due consideration of human imperfection, that the best things of the world are those in which the least ill intervenes.

Judging according to the common nature and the universal customs of man, although I would not dare assert it, yet I believe that love among men is not only not reprehensible but almost necessary, and a true enough demonstration of gentility and greatness of soul.[4] And above all it invites men to worthy and excellent things and induces them to exercise and bring into action those virtues which are in the soul potentially. For he who diligently searches what may be the true definition of love finds it to be no other than the appetite for beauty.[5] And if this be so, then all deformed and ugly things are necessarily unpleasant to the lover.

Putting aside for the moment that love which according to Plato is the means for all things to find their perfection and ultimately to rest in supreme Beauty, which is God, and speaking of that love which extends only to the loving of the human creature,[6] I say that although this is not that perfec-

4. The earlier courtly notion of the *dolce stil novo* concerning *"gentilezza"* was echoed by Ficino in his discussion of that desire for beauty and nobility which attracts man to loving what is excellent. Cf. *Sopra lo Amore*, I, 3, or the Latin text of his commentary on the *Symposium*, I, 4 and *Symposium*, 178, d–e. In succeeding references to Ficino, reference to the Italian text will precede reference to the Latin, the latter in parentheses.

5. Ficino, I, 3 (I, 4) and II, 9 (II, 9).

6. The distinction between heavenly and earthly love is clear in Ficino when he speaks of the two Venuses and two Cupids, II, 7 (II, 7). Cf. *Symposium*, 180, d–181, d.

tion of love which is called "the highest good," at least we see clearly that it contains in itself a great many goods and avoids a great many ills. So according to the common custom of human life it holds the place of the good, above all if it is accompanied by those circumstances and conditions which are fitting to a real lover. These seem to me to be two: the first is that one loves only one thing, and the second that one loves such a thing always. These two conditions can come to ill if the loved subject does not have in itself the highest perfection in proportion with other human things, and that in addition to natural beauties the loved one not combine great genius, honest and well-adorned habits and customs, elegant gestures and manner, skill with wise and sweet words, love, constancy and faith. All these things necessarily come together in the perfection of love because, although the beginning of love is born from the eyes[7] and from beauty, nonetheless those other conditions are necessary for its conservation and continuance. For if either by illness or age or other reasons the face should lose its color and beauty should be lacking either in whole or in part, then all those other conditions remain no less pleasing to the soul and to the heart than beauty to the eyes. Nor would these conditions be yet sufficient if there were not in the lover the real understanding of this condition, which presupposes perfection of judgment in the lover; nor could there be the love of the loved one toward the lover if he who loves did not merit being loved, and thus the infallible judgment of the loved one is presupposed.

Thus he who proposes a true love of necessity proposes great perfection, according to the common customs of men, both in the loved one and in the lover. And, as happens with

7. As with the notion of *"gentilezza,"* the origin of love in the eyes was a topic well established in the *dolce stil novo* again taken up by Ficino, II, 9 (II, 9) and passim.

all other perfect things, I think that such a love has been very rare in the world—and this argues its excellence all the more. He who loves a single thing and loves it always, necessarily does not place his love in other things, and yet he gets rid of all the errors and voluptuous pleasures which men commonly incur. In loving a person whom it is fitting to know and in searching to please that person in every way he can, it is necessarily required that in all his works he try to dignify himself and make himself excellent among the others, following virtuous works in order as much as he can to make himself worthy of her whom he esteems most worthy above all others. As there appears always present in his heart both openly and hiddenly the form of the loved one, so it should be present in all his works, which he will praise or criticize as is appropriate accordingly as it is the real witness and assisting judge not only of his work but also of his thoughts. And so, partly by shame repressing evil and partly by the stimulus to please urging the good, such lovers will always, even if they do not achieve perfection, at least do what is held not bad in the world, and what with respect to human imperfection is well chosen.

This then has been the subject of my poems. If, even with all this discussion, I do not respond to the accusations and calumnies of those who would harm me, at least "I hope to find pity, if not pardon," as our Florentine poet said it,[8] among those who have experienced what love is;[9] and their judgment is enough for my satisfaction. For if it is true, as Guido Guinizelli says, that love and gentleness of heart turn the one into the other and are one single thing,[10] then I believe that the praise of high and gentle minds would be

8. Petrarca, *Rime* I, 8: "spero trovar pietà, se non perdono."

9. Cf. Petrarca, *Rime* I, 7.

10. Guido Guinizelli (*ca.* 1230–1276), traditionally the initiator of the *dolce stil novo;* the poem referred to begins: "Al cor gentil ripara sempre Amore" (Love always takes shelter in the gentle heart).

enough for men, and that they should desire only this, for it is impossible to do anything in this world that would be praised by all men. Thus the man of discernment tries to gather praise from those who are themselves worthy of it and who care little for the opinions of others. It seems to me that one cannot blame what is natural: nothing is more natural than the appetite to join oneself to what is beautiful, and this appetite was ordained in men by nature, for the propagation of mankind which is necessary to the continuing of the human race. What ought to move us to this true reason is not nobility of blood, or hope for possessions, for riches or other advantage, but only the unforced natural choice, unconcerned in any other regard and moved only by a certain conformity and proportion that the loved one and the lover have in common to the end of propagating the human race. Those are then completely to be condemned whom the appetite moves to loving completely those things which are beyond this natural order and true end which we have proposed. Those are to be praised who in pursuing this end love one single thing lastingly and with firm constancy and faith.

It seems to me that the objection has been met fully enough. And given that this love of which we have spoken is good, it does not seem very necessary to purge that part of me which would seem more than blameworthy because of my various public and private responsibilities; for, if it is good, the good has no need of any excuses, for it has no fault. Yet if some scrupulous judge should not want to allow these arguments, at least let him concede this small license to young and tender age, which seems not to owe so much to the censure and judgment of men and in which any error seems less serious; and in particular, more stimulated as youth is to deviate from the direct way through lack of experience, one can hardly oppose those things which are nature and common custom among others. I say this in case it should be held an error to love greatly with much sincerity and faith something which by its own perfection forces the love of the lover. If this is so, either for the reasons stated or because of age, neither the composition nor the commenting of my poems which had been done in this sense can be held a serious error in me. Given it were true that commentary is not appropriate to such material, insofar as it is minor and unimportant either to the edification or the happiness of our mind, I say that if this is the case then the task of this commentary is most appropriately mine, so that a more excellent mind than mine should not have to occupy itself or spend time on such lowly things. Yet if the material is high and worthy, as it seems to me, then explaining it well and making it plain and intelligible is useful to everyone. For both this reason and that one which I have stated above, no one can do it with a clearer setting forth of the true meaning than I myself. Moreover I am not the first to comment on verses that contain similar subjects of love, for Dante himself commented upon some of his canzoni and other poems.[11] And I have read the commentaries of Egidio Romano and of Dino del Garbo,[12] both excellent philosophers, upon that very subtle canzone of Guido Cavalacanti, a man esteemed in his time the best dialectician in the world, a man of excellence in addition to these vernacular verses of his, as is shown in his other works but above all in the above-mentioned canzone, which begins "Donna mi prega" and concerns nothing other than the beginning of how love is born in gentle hearts and its effects.[13] Yet if neither the arguments nor the examples above are sufficient to my justification, compassion at least

11. In the *Vita Nuova*, Dante traces his love for Beatrice in sonnets linked with prose commentary; in the *Convivio* he comments upon three canzoni.

12. Egidio Colonna Romano (Aegidius Romanus Eremita, 1246–1316), theologian, student of Aquinas and author of the *De regimine principum.* Dino del Garbo (d. 1327), Florentine physician and philosopher.

13. Cavalcanti (*ca.* 1255–1300), friend of Dante, was a strong sympathizer of the Guelphs and opponent of the Donati family, see *Purg.*, XI, 57–98 and *Inf.*, X, 60 ff.

ought to clear me, for since in my youth I was much sought out both by men and by fortune, then some small rest ought not to be denied me. I have found it only in loving and in the composition and commenting of my poems, as we shall make more clearly understood when we come to the exposition of the sonnet which begins, "Se tra gli altri sospir ch'escon di fòre." It is impossible for others to understand what consolation and what respite my gentle and constant love gave to those evil persecutions, which are quite public and well known.[14] For when I had told it to anyone, it was as impossible for him to understand as for me to tell the truth about them. However, I return to the above-mentioned verse of our Florentine poet, that wherever there may be one who by experience understands love (thus this love which I have so much praised as much as some particular love and charity concerning me), "I hope to find pity if not pardon."[15]

There remains then only to reply to the possible objection of writing in the vernacular, which according to some is not capable or worthy of any excellent material and subject. To this I reply that nothing can be the less worthy for being common; on the contrary, one finds every good to be so much the better insofar as it is communicable and universal. Such is by nature what is called "the highest Good," for it would not be highest if it were not infinite, nor can any thing be called "infinite" if not what is common to everything.

Thus it does not seem that dignity is taken away from our mother tongue by its being common to all of Italy, but one must in fact think about the perfection or imperfection of that language. Having considered what are those conditions

14. Lorenzo alludes to the conspiracy against the Medici known as the *Congiura de' Pazzi*. The Pazzi family attacked Lorenzo and Giuliano de' Medici in the Duomo of Florence; Giuliano was killed, Lorenzo escaped and a number of the conspirators were executed.

15. See note 8 above.

that give dignity or perfection to any tongue or language whatsoever, I seem to find four: of these one or at most two would be true and proper and praiseworthy qualities of the language; the others depend more either upon the customs and opinion of men or upon fortune. What is truly praiseworthy in a language is its fullness and abundance and its being apt for expressing well the mental sense and concept. Thus the Greek language is judged more perfect than the Latin and the Latin better than the Hebrew, for the one expresses better than the other the mind of the speaker or writer. The other condition which dignifies a language is the sweetness and harmony that result in one more than another; and although harmony is natural and is proportionate to the harmony of the soul and our bodies, nonetheless it seems to me, because of the variety of human minds, that if not everyone is well proportioned and perfect, yet this is more a matter of opinion than of reason. For those things which are judged according to whether they are commonly pleasing or not seem founded rather upon opinion than upon real reason, particularly those of which the pleasure or displeasure is not experienced otherwise than through the appetite. And yet, these reasons notwithstanding, I do not want to claim that this cannot be praiseworthy of the language proper because, as I have said, harmony being proportionate to human nature, one can infer the judgment that the sweetness of such harmony conforms to those who are similarly well proportioned to receive it; and the judgment of these ought to be accepted as good, even though they be [few].[16] For the pronouncements and judgments of men should sooner be weighed than enumerated.

The other condition which makes a language excellent is

16. I accept the emendation suggested by Bigi, p. 307 of his edition, and thus add the word.

when there are written in it things subtle and weighty and necessary to human life, both for the mind and for human action and bodily well-being. This we can say of the Hebrew, for it contains wonderful mysteries, which are suited or rather necessary to the infallible truth of our faith; and similarly of the Greek, which contains much metaphysical, natural and moral knowledge very necessary to the human race. And when we come to this, we must confess that it is more the subject than the language which is worthy, because the subject is the end and the language the means. Thus that language cannot be called more perfect in itself, for it is the greater perfection of the material treated in it which is judged. When one has written of theology, metaphysics, natural and moral philosophy, then as far as his language may be concerned it seems that praise is reserved more for the material than not, and that the language would have served the role of an instrument to be judged good or bad according to its end.

There remains a single other condition that gives stature to a language. This is when things happen in such a way as to make universal and more or less common to all the world what is naturally proper to one city or province. This can be more easily considered as prosperity of fortune than a real value of the language itself, because a language is prized and widely celebrated in the world according to the opinions of those men who prize and esteem it. One cannot call truly and properly good what depends upon others than itself, for those who prize it could easily disprize it and change their opinion. And so too the conditions could change, and in the absence of the cause the dignity and worthiness of the language would be lacking. Such a dignity of having been praised because of prosperity and success according to fortune is very much the case of the Latin language, for the spread of the Roman Empire made it not only common but also virtually necessary in all the world.

Thus we conclude that these external praises of the language, which depend upon the opinion of others or upon fortune, are not proper values of the language itself. On that account, in our desire to show the dignity of our own language, we must insist solely upon the first conditions: whether our language easily expresses any concept whatsoever of our thoughts. To this end, no better reason can be introduced than that of experience. Dante, Petrarca and Boccaccio, our Florentine poets, have clearly shown themselves capable in their weighty and sweet verses and orations of expressing all meaning with great facility. He who reads Dante's *Commedia* will find in it many natural and theological things expressed with great skill and ease; he will also find very suitably adopted in the writing those three kinds of style which are praised by the orators, the humble, the middle and the high. In effect, Dante has perfectly brought to completion in one style what is found in various authors, both Greek and Latin. Who will then deny that in Petrarca is found a weighty style, polished and sweet, and that he treats the things of love with a gravity and grace such as is not to be found in Ovid, Tibullus, Catullus and Propertius or any other Latin poet?[17] Dante's canzoni and sonnets are so grave, subtle and ornate that they are virtually unmatched in prose. He who has read Boccaccio, such a learned and eloquent man, will easily judge not only the invention but also the fullness and eloquence of his work to be unique in the world. And, when one considers his *Decameron,* doubtless he will judge no language better than ours in aptness of expression. For the material of that book is varied, now grave, now middle and now low; it contains all the troubles that can befall man from love and from hatred, from fear and from hope, as well as so many new tricks and ingenious expedients;

17. Cf. Ovid's comments on Propertius, Tibullus and Catullus in *Tristia,* V, i., 17, *Amores,* I, xv, 28 and *Amores,* III, ix, 62.

and its subject is the expression of all the natures and passions of men on earth. Guido Cavalcanti, whom we have already mentioned, combined gravity and sweetness indescribably well, as shown by the canzone discussed above and by some of his sonnets and ballades.[18]

There remain yet many other weighty and elegant writers, whom we shall leave aside more in order to avoid extended discussion than because they are not worthy of it. Yet we shall conclude that men have been lacking to exercise the language rather than that the language has not been sufficient to the men and material. The sweetness and harmony of it is truly very great and appropriate to great things, so long as one takes some care with it in order to become accustomed to it.

In our language there seem to me plenty of these things which are the proper praiseworthy qualities of language, and perhaps it may appear so to someone else. Because up to the present Dante and his work have been treated above all, it seems to me not only useful but also necessary that his verses be read for their serious and important effects, as shown by the example of many commentaries written upon his *Commedia* by learned and famous men and by the frequent citations of him on the part of holy and excellent men,[19] as we hear every day in their public preaching. Perhaps there will be yet other subtle and important things, worthy of being read, written in this language, since it is constantly becoming more elegant and courteous. And it could easily in its youth and adulthood come to even greater perfection and successful prospering and increase to the Florentine empire, as one ought not only to hope but also to assist with all the intelligence and power of good citizens. Yet this, which is in the power of fortune and in the will of the ineffable judg-

18. Cf. note 13 above.

19. Lorenzo probably alludes particularly to Landino; cf. the end of the selection from Landino, pp. 128–129 above.

ment of God, is not to be despaired of, even though it is not good to affirm it. At present, let the following conclusion suffice: our language abounds in those worthy qualities which are properly of a language; and we cannot justly complain about it. For these same reasons, no one can criticize me if I have written in that language in which I was born and raised, above all because Hebrew and Greek and Latin were in their own times natural mother tongues; but they were spoken and written more accurately with some rules and reason by those who are honored and praised for it than by the common people and the crowd.

13

Giovanni Pico della Mirandola

PRAISE OF LORENZO (AND CRITIQUE OF DANTE AND PETRARCA)[1]

I have read, Lorenzo, the poetry which the vernacular Muses inspired in you at a tender age. I recognized a legitimate offspring of the Muses and Graces, but I did not recognize a youthful work. For who would not perceive the Graces dancing rhythmically in your harmonious compositions? Who would not hear the Muses singing in your melodious expression? Who would recognize a young man in your unstudied grace, lively wit, honeyed facetiousness, apt charms, wonderful naturalness, judicious arrangement and grave thoughts drawn from the secrets of philosophy? I know that I am certainly in no position to judge such things; but I wish what I think about them could be said without my being suspected of flattery. I should certainly say that there is no one of the old writers whom you have not surpassed by a long distance; and lest you think I have said this to curry favor, I shall tell you my reasons for this opinion.

You have two especially celebrated poets of the Florentine tongue, Francesco Petrarca and Dante Alighieri, about whom let me say this by way of general preface: There are some learned men who find Petrarca defective in content, Dante in style. No one with mind and ears would find you defective in

1. Translated from *Prosatori Latini del Quattrocento*.

either: it is hard to say whether your subject is more illumined by your language, or your words by your thoughts. But let us weigh, one by one—as if in a balance—the merits of each.

If Petrarca should come back to life, is there any doubt that where thought is concerned he would give the palm to you? You are always so acute, grave and subtle, whereas he generally seizes his thoughts where he can find them and applies a verbal coloring: he renders the common extraordinary by his mode of expression. Let us see in what respect he excels you stylistically, and you him. In some places I'll grant he appears more charming; but I find his charm sweetly sour and pleasantly severe. He is diffuse and uniformly captivating, while you seize our minds with a majesty and a certain vigorous splendor of language. His diligence is ostentatious and excessive; yours, careless rather than studied. He is tender and gentle; you are bold and muscular. He is flowing and melodious, you are concise, rich, firm and modulated. He is perhaps more elegant, you are certainly more dignified and lofty. He is more beautified, but you are more vigorous. In him there is something you'd cut away, in you there is nothing superfluous and nothing incomplete. Perhaps I am being a bit presumptuous, saying that something should be removed from him, but it is certainly so: it seems so to many, on whose judgment I rely (for in my own I have no confidence). One can often see him committing the same fault the Asiatics committed,[2] that is, stuffing in words as though to fill cracks, employing sonorous and striking sounds not to adorn his poem but to prop it up, so that it will not limp. All your words are no less necessary to express the subject than they are pleasing in the embellishment of it. Taking anything

2. On the Asiatic style of oratory, see Cicero, *Brutus,* 325; and *Orator,* 25, and especially 231 (the source of Pico's remark about "stuffing in words as though to fill cracks").

away from you would be mutilation; from him, pruning and cleansing. But even if we should grant (and I never will) that his writings are more elegant and embellished than yours, that was an easy performance for a man who did not have to struggle with thoughts themselves. It can hardly be said how your penetrating, subtle and—to put it in a word— Laurentian thoughts reject artificial ornaments and do not willingly receive those rouges. Reading Petrarca we find him delicate, polished, pleasing; but if he had had to handle your thoughts, we should find him crabbed, rude and unpleasing, for you can see that whenever he approaches any such thing he is shrill, entangled or knotty: his style falls as the thought rises. When he displays that verbal baggage of his, his perfumes and beautiful ornaments, if Castritius were present he would often give the same warning he gave with reference to Gracchus, that we not be deceived by a resounding flow of verses, but examine what is underneath, what foundation the words have.[3] Do this and you would sometimes see there the void of Epicurus: either no meaning underneath, or a feeble and trivial one. In this very important respect, even if you do not excel Petrarca, I do not see at all why he excels you in grace of expression, since your words could not be more illustrious, and their collocation is so apt that they could in no way hold together better or flow more smoothly or fall more harmoniously.

But now let us weigh Dante with you. Many perhaps would quarrel about him, for there are lots of people who in comparing writers do not so much reckon merits as count years: they bid others read the old writers with reverence while they themselves cannot read contemporary writers without ill-will. With regard to style, I am sure no one will deny you primacy; Dante is sometimes rough, harsh and dry, and very rude and unpolished. This even his supporters

3. Aulus Gellius, *Noctes Atticae*, XI, xiii.

admit, but they cast the blame for his being so upon his times. You are altogether more elegant in language, and he is not loftier. But, they will say, he is loftier and more sublime in his thoughts. Pray tell me, what is wonderful about his philosophizing on a philosophical subject, which by its very nature forced him to do so and of itself supplied his thoughts? If he deals with God, the soul and the blessed, he repeats what Thomas and Augustine wrote on these subjects, which he pondered and meditated upon constantly and assiduously. Then again, in recounting great matters public and private, it was not so splendid of Dante to have done this as it would have been shameful not to. But what you offer was undoubtedly a work of the highest genius, to make amatory themes philosophical and, by covering them with charm, make lovely things that are somewhat harsh because of their own severity. In your verses the serious themes of philosophers are so mixed with lovers' games that the latter have gained grandeur and the former gaiety and grace. By this bond both have retained what was their own and also shared mutually, so that each has singly what previously belonged to them separately. But this is not as admirable as that which has most impressed me: these things are conveyed by you in such fashion that they seem not conveyed but drawn from the bosom of the material itself—flowering forth from it, so to speak, while you just watered the ground—so that they appear native, not foreign; inevitable, not prepared; natural, not engrafted. It is in this, which I cannot admire sufficiently, that you seem to me to have surpassed Dante. For even if he flies aloft, he is lifted up on the wings of his subject matter, whereas your subject resists and draws you downward; you are borne on high by the wings of genius, and so borne that you do not forsake your subject matter but lift it up together with you. Your subject owes you as much as Dante owed his subject.

Now one can see what difference there is between you and

Petrarca and Dante. About them I would add this, that Petrarca sometimes does not answer up to his promises; he has that which entices at first sight but does not satisfy further, whereas Dante has that which on contact is sometimes annoying but pleases more as you search out its profundities. Your poetry has no less in its secret recesses to engage the reader, than it has in its exterior appearance to captivate him. In addition, they wrote their poetry in solitary retreats, at leisure, in the deepest studious tranquility; you wrote yours while extremely busy, amidst violent commotions, the noise of the curia and the din of the forum, amid weighty cares and troubled times. To them the Muses were their ordinary and principal employment; to you, an amusement and a relaxation from cares. To them it was extremely exhausting toil; to you, repose when you were exhausted. In short, relaxing your mind you reached where they perhaps did not reach by exerting all their mental powers. . . .[4]

4. The letter concludes with a discussion of Lorenzo's *Commentary*.

IV.

CINQUECENTO EPILOGUE

14

PIETRO BEMBO

THE EVALUATION OF VERNACULAR COMPOSITIONS[1]

My lord Giulio, all wise men agree that there are in the life of man two ways, by traveling along which he may arrive at great praise of himself along with great usefulness to others. One of these is the doing of fine and laudable things; the other the considering and contemplating not only of what man can do but also of those things God has done, their causes and effects and their order, and above all contemplating Him their maker and disposer and keeper, God. For with good works, both in peace and in war, one brings pleasure in various ways to private persons, to communities of people and to nations; and through contemplation man becomes wise and prudent, and can do the same for others who abound in much virtue, by showing them what he has found and considered. Each of these two ways was so much praised in itself by the ancient philosophers that the question is still hanging today which of them one ought to advance, and

1. The participants in the dialogue are Bembo's brother Carlo (d. 1503), Giuliano de' Medici (1479–1516, third son of Lorenzo), Federico Fregoso (d. 1541, archbishop of Salerno in 1507 and cardinal in 1539) and Ercole Strozzi (*ca.* 1473–1508). The fictional date of the dialogue is 1502; the dedication in the first book is written as if from 1515; the book was presented in manuscript to Clement VII in 1524 and published in 1525. Translated from the *Prose della volgar lingua*, Book II, Chapters 1–8, in Bembo, *Prose e Rime*, ed. Carlo Dionisotti (Turin, 1966).

which is better. Now if the pen had been lacking with regard to good works and fine contemplations, and had no one written them, they would not have been of such duration as they are. Since there has been taken from them the possibility of being understood by all people, and for many centuries, they would give pleasure neither in the example nor in the teaching, unless in the slightest way to the extent that memory and written testimony can accomplish. When these are commended attractively and gaily, they not only offer great fruit but also bring marvelous delight to human minds, which are always naturally fond of understanding and knowledge. For this reason were written infinite things first by the Egyptians, an infinity then by the Phoenicians, the Assyrians, the Chaldeans, and by other nations after these; an infinity above all by the Greeks, who were great and diligent masters of all the sciences and disciplines and of all ways of writing; finally, an infinity by the Romans, who rivaled the Greeks for literary supremacy, thinking to conquer them, as they had in the arts of horsemanship and governing, in this field where they advanced so far that the Latin language has become such as we see it.

Now, my lord Giulio, and in these last centuries the vernacular language is winning out over the Latin, and it has succeeded so fortunately that already excellent if few writers are to be read, both in prose and in verse. For beginning with that century leading up to Dante, straightaway arose many vernacular poets, not only in your city and all of Tuscany, but also elsewhere.[2] There were for example Piero delle Vigne, Buonagiunta da Lucca, Guittone d'Arezzo, Rinaldo d'Acquino, Lapo Gianni, Francesco Ismera, Forese Donati,

2. After discussing the Provençal poets in the first book (I, 8 ff.) , Bembo here lists the Sicilian and Italian poets of the twelfth and thirteenth centuries.

Gianni Alfani, Ser Brunetto, Jacomo da Lentino the Notary, Mazzeo and Guido Giudice of Messina, King Enzo, Emperor Federigo, Onesto and Semprebene da Bologna, Guido Guinicelli also of Bologna, who was much praised by Dante, Lupo degli Uberti, who was a rather fine and faultless poet for that time, Guido Orlandi, Guido Cavalcanti. We read today compositions by all these men. And Guido Ghisilieri, and Fabruzio from Bologna, Gallo of Pisa, Gotto of Mantua who had Dante listen to his songs, Nino of Siena, and others whose writings, as far as I know, we do not read today. There came close to these, and together with some of them, Dante, great and magnificent poet, who left them all far behind. Close to Dante, in fact of his generation, although he outlived him, came Cino, a poet who was charming and courteous and above all amorous and sweet, but in fact of much less talent; and Dino Frescobaldi, also a quite famous poet of that time, and Jacopo Alighieri, son of Dante, much the lesser and less renowned than either his father or Dino. Petrarca followed these, and one sees in him gathered all the graces of vernacular poetry. In those times there were likewise many writers of prose, of all of whom Giovanni Villani, who lived at the time of Dante and wrote the history of Florence, is not to be slighted; and much less Pietro Crescenzo of Bologna, older than Villani, whose twelve books concerning the needs of the rural life we have to hand. And of those who wrote in verse, some also wrote in prose, such as Guido Giudice of Messina, and Dante himself, and others. But each of them was defeated and surpassed by Boccaccio, and he by himself, since among his many compositions, each one was better according to the distance of its birth from his youth. Although Boccaccio also composed many pieces in verse, nonetheless one recognizes him quite evidently to have been born for prose. After these writers there have been many in both the one faculty and the other. Nevertheless, one sees that the great growth of lan-

guage was the task of these two alone, Petrarca and Boccaccio; from then to the present, one sees no writer yet who
surpasses or even arrives at the same level as these two. This
will surely be drawn to the shame of our century; for now
that the Latin language has been purged so thoroughly of the
rust from those unlearned past centuries that it has today
recovered its ancient splendor and delightfulness, it does not
seem right that this language which we can compare to one
newborn should so soon be halted, to go no further forward.
For this reason I urge our men to give themselves over to
writing in the vernacular, since it is our language, as was said
in those things told and gathered in the first book. For with
what language can one more conveniently and more easily
write than with the one with which we speak? With this
as a goal, and in order that men be given greater ease in
such matters, I shall in this second book set out the discussion
of the second day, carried on among those people of whom we
spoke in the first book.

Thus the three had returned, after having eaten, to the
house of my brother as they had planned; and since the north
wind, which was still blowing, made it cold, they gathered
round the fire and when each had warmed up they sat down
along with my brother. Then after they had rested a bit,
Giuliano began to speak to the others thus: "I do not know if
the great desire I have that messer Ercole should be disposed
to writing and composition in the vernacular has brought it
about that last night I saw a dream, or whether there has
been at work some virtue of the heavens or perhaps of our
souls, which sometimes make men see things as they are to
come, before they happen, by this path. I am sooner inclined
to believe the latter, but however that may be, I do want to
tell you about the dream. As I said, while I was sleeping last
night I seemed to be on a very beautiful bank of the Arno,
shaded with many laurels and entirely covered with grass and

flowers right down to the pure and high water which bathed it, running with pleasant languor. And it seemed to me that all over the river, as far as my eyes could reach, the whitest of swans were going about in pleasant diversions. Some of them, which were many everywhere, were moving upstream, using their webbed feet against the river in the manner of oars; some in accord with the flow of the beautiful water let themselves be carried by it, moving themselves little; and others, in the middle of the river or near the green banks, were playing and receiving the sun which made them perfectly pure. From all of them was heard come forth such sweet song and pleasing harmony that the river and the banks and all the air and every thing round about seemed full of infinite delight. And while I was feeding my eyes and ears on that sight and that harmony, a perfectly white and very large swan that was coming through the air from the left side, lowering its flight slowly, softly came to rest in the middle of the river; and this one too began to sing, rendering strange and sweet melody. It seemed that all the others gave honor to this bird, showing joy at his coming and making a wide crown of their flocks about him. While I was marveling at this and searching for its reason, it was said to me, I know not by whom, that this swan which I saw had once been a very beautiful youth, son of the Po, and that those others similarly had been men, as I was. But this one who, having changed form in the lap of his father and passing in flight to the Tiber had made the banks of that river resound with his voices for a good length of time, now had come to the Arno and desired to reside there for as much time. Thus the others were making a marvelous celebration, one and all knowing how melodious and courteous he was.[3] My sleep then shortly left me. Thinking over the dream and the present state of messer Ercole, I

3. The swan is Ercole Strozzi, born at Ferrara on the Po River; the swans of the Arno are the Florentine poets. Strozzi wrote Latin poetry while at Rome and late in his life did convert to writing in the vernacular.

now take hope that persuaded by us he may shortly turn his study back to the vernacular and with it write many things as perfectly as those he has written in Latin. For this reason I am set to be quiet about nothing I know which he may ask of me, as yesterday he said he wished to do. And I urge you to do the like, messer Federigo and messer Carlo. Thus the three of us together may adopt every care that may be to his profit."

"Let us do so," said messer Federigo immediately. "And may there be nothing lacking on our part. One must do it all the more willingly, as Giuliano's dream invites us, for I take it as a pledge and already seem to see messer Ercole, passing from the Roman to the Florentine Muses, almost as if he had become a swan, sending forth new songs and spreading through the air the most gentle harmony and sweetness."

Then my brother said, "Messer Federigo, Strozzi can give himself over to writing in the vernacular as easily as you think, for I have no less faith in Giuliano's dream than you. If he does this, then surely he will seem not even so much a swan as a phoenix,[4] his rare and happy genius will carry him through the sky in such a way. For I wish I knew how to urge him not to fail himself, and as far as it pertains to me, I will assist him in it willingly if I can know how or when to do it."

"You do me too much honor," said Strozzi in reply, "for I do not dare to desire [such things] nor do I consider it would be appropriate to me. And Giuliano's dream, which is truly a dream in all its parts, could perhaps be prophetic only in this—that I may write in the vernacular some time, if I live long enough. Since just a short while ago, I have felt so much desire for doing it, as a consequence of your persuasions, that

---

4. Phoenix: i.e., unique. Cf. Petrarca, *Rime,* CCX, 4: "Né 'n ciel, né 'n terra è più d'una fenice" (Neither in heaven nor on earth is there but one phoenix).

it will be no marvel if I try at some time or other to draw from it some will to act. But to return to our questions of yesterday, which we have come here today to investigate, I would like to ask a question of you, messer Carlo.[5] You said to us that the writer when writing must choose and follow that manner which is best, whether it be classical and of deceased men or modern and of our own writers; I would like to know how and with what rules one may judge this and know the good writer from the bad, and which is greater and which less among the good ones; and finally, why must one believe, concerning this same form of composition we spoke of yesterday, that present Tuscan writers are not so good as Boccaccio and Petrarca?"

"To reply briefly," said my brother, "it is because in one case the form has its highly praised writers and in the other not. For since as you know each writer receives praise according to how good he is, so it comes about that one can make an easy argument for value. Thus among Greek writers, one sees no other poet or orator of such repute as Homer or Demosthenes; and among the Latins, there is no one so completely praised as Virgil and Cicero. Thus it can be said that they are better writers—as they are—than all the rest. Similarly I speak, messer Ercole, of our future vernacular. For since among all the Tuscan writers of verse and prose there is no one whose manner of writing surpasses or even matches that of the two whom you have mentioned, so one ought then to believe that their modes of writing are better than any

5. The initial question of the first book is how to evaluate one language over another, given the diversity of human speech. The discussion turns finally to the problems of ennobling the Italian vernacular, and concludes that contemporary popular usage is not adequate to enrich a language but that the writers must imitate and learn from better writers, whether these be of the past or present, of the same or another language. As Petrarca and Boccaccio used classical writers to enrich the language, and not Dante, so the contemporary of Bembo would use Petrarca and Boccaccio, but not the coarse writings of present-day writers.

others. Furthermore, if someone should also wish, without putting his mind to the fame of writers, to take sense from their writings and to give them meaning, certainly this can be done by diligently considering all the parts of the writings in question; and in doing so one may get a more certain and secure experience of them than in another way. The reason is that it may well happen that someone may live who would be a better poet or orator than any of the ancients, and nonetheless have not so much repute or fame gathered from the people as they have. For repute does not come equally quickly to every writer, and they are very few who have had as much in their lifetimes as they deserved."

"Messer Carlo," said Strozzi, "what now are those parts which you say are to be considered by whoever wants to draw this judgment from them?"

"They are in great part those that one considers also in Latin composition," replied my brother. "And it is not my business to gather them for you, since they are clearer and better known to you than to me. Concerning the others, which are thus not many, we shall see, if you would like us to search them out."

Strozzi said, "I do not want you to look into what may be clear or not to me in the Latin language, for I might lose by it; and you might find me a great deal less a connoisseur than by chance you think. And I do not want you to separate those parts of vernacular speech which fall equally in the Latin from those that do not, since it could easily be more difficult to make this choice than to set forth the whole sum. But what I am looking for—and I entreat you and charge you with it—is for you, without any regard for the Latin, to tell me what all those parts are that allow one in considering the question I have raised to make that judgment and to draw out that meaning which you are talking about."

"Messer Ercole," replied my brother, "I do not know whether I can now gather together all of them, which are surely many, individually and minutely considered. But in general they are these: the material or subject which we intend, about which one writes, and the form or appearance that one gives to the material, and that is to say the writing. But because we spoke yesterday and are again talking today among ourselves not of the material with regard to which anyone writes, but of the way in which one writes, then I, speaking of this second part, say that every manner of writing is composed of two parts. One of these is the choice, the second the disposition, of the words;[6] thus first one investigates with what words we may more suitably write what we have undertaken and next it is our task to consider with what order and composition and harmony of them, these same words may correspond better than in another manner. For neither is every word of the many with which one may signify a thing equally grave or pure or sweet, nor does every arrangement of those same words have the same enhancement, or please or delight in the same way. Thus if one is speaking of great material, the words to be chosen are weighty, elevated, resounding, clear and glowing; if of low and vulgar material, then light, plain, humble, popular and quiet; if of the mean between these two, then similarly with intermediate and temperate words, and those which tend the least possible to one or the other of these two extremes.[7] And it is no less part of the business in these rules to keep the style and to avoid satiety, varying from time to time both the weighty words with some temperate ones and the temperate with some light, and so vice versa these latter with some of the others neither more nor less. Always the general and uni-

---

6. Cf. Caesar, *Brutus*, LXXII, 253, Cicero, *De Oratore*, III, xxxvii, 149, and Quintilian, *Instit. Orat.*, X, iii, 5.
7. Cf. Cicero, *De Orat.*, III, xxix, 100–101.

versal rule is to choose and bring into our compositions as much as possible the most pure, the most spotless, always the most clear, the most beautiful and the most pleasing words. How one does this would be long to discuss, for these very same words are either properly of the things one is talking about, and seem as if born together with them, or they are drawn from likenesses of other things to which they are related and are placed in the relation to what we are speaking of or are newly made and formed by us.[8] And these words then thus divided and set in parts, have other parts and other divisions under them, which are all to be known. But you can learn that from those who write of it in Latin.

And yet it may happen some time that what we propose to write cannot be expressed in proper words and it is necessary to have recourse to low or harsh or contemptible ones. I can only barely believe this possible, since there are so many ways and modes of talking and human language is so variable and serviceable in taking diverse forms and appearances and colors, so to speak. But if nonetheless it happens, I say one should keep quiet about that part which cannot be expressed properly, rather than mar the other writing in expressing it.[9] This ought to be done particularly where necessity does not constrain or force the writer, and that sort of necessity touches poets least of all writers. Your own Dante, Giuliano, when he wanted to make comparisons about the scabious ones, would have done better to have kept quiet about all of it than to write in the way he did:

> *E non vidi già mai menare stregghia*
> *a ragazzo aspettato da signorso*
> (And I never saw wield a currycomb
> a boy awaited by his master)

8. Cf. Cicero, *De Orat.*, III, xxxvii, 149.
9. Cf. Horace, *Ars Poetica*, 149–150.

and shortly thereafter:[10]

> *E si traevan giù l'unghie la scabbia*
> *come coltel di scardova le scaglie.*
> (And their nails were pulling down the scabs
> as a knife the scales of a carp.)

There are many things of this sort that could have been passed over by him without blame, for no necessity constrained him rather to write them than not, where it is not blameless that they are said. If that poet had not said what cannot be said properly, he would have done better both in this and in many other places of his compositions; and moreover, if he had been willing to take the trouble to say with more pleasing and honorable words what can be said after some thought, but which he said coarsely and dishonorably, then he would have had much greater fame and praise, no matter how much he may have. And when he said

> *Biscazza, e fonde la sua facultate*
> (Gambles, and wastes his wealth)

he should have said 'consumes' or 'scatters' and not 'gambles,' a word completely harsh and unpleasant; furthermore, it is not a word used in literature and perhaps has never been touched by other writers.[11] Petrarca did not do things this way; let us leave aside that he never took to saying what cannot be said properly, for among things said well, if there was any minute word which could be said better, he would change it and change it again, until it could not be said better in any way whatsoever."

Giuliano, interposing here, turned toward Strozzi and said: "How true it is, messer Ercole, what Bembo tells us of

---

10. *Inf.*, XXIX, 76–77, 82–83.

11. *Inf.*, XI, 44. Bembo does not seem to understand the meaning of *"biscazza"*; he appears nonetheless to be correct in observing that the word is not used by other writers.

Petrarca in this regard. For not long ago I saw several pages
written in the poet's own hand,[12] in which there were a good
number of his poems; and in those leaves he showed how he
annotated them as he went about composing them, some
entire, some cut short, some in great part struck out and
changed many times. I read among the others these two
verses first written in this way:

> *Voi, ch'ascoltate in rime sparse il suono*
> *di quei sospir, de' quai nutriva il core.*[13]

Then he must have thought that saying *'de' quai nutriva il*
core' was not full enough, but that it lacked the person and
in addition that the proximity of that other phrase *'di quei'*
detracted from the grace of this *'de' quai';* so he changed it
and made of it *'di ch'io nutriva il core.'* Finally, remember-
ing the word *onde,* which is more round and sonorous and
full with its two consonants, and adding the thought that
saying *'sospiri'* is a more complete word and more pleasing
than *'sospir,'* he chose to say it thus, as one reads now rather
than otherwise. But continue, messer Carlo."

Messer Carlo took up his discussion again as follows:
"Words can have many other aspects that diminish their
grace. For sometimes they can be loose and languid beyond
what is appropriate, or dense and compressed, fat or dry,
delicate or coarse, taciturn or raucous, and sluggish or quick,
paralyzed and slippery, and out of fashion both when old and
when new. Thus the poet who guards himself better from
these and similar defects and writes better works out of good

---

12. Bembo edited the *Rime* of Petrarca from autograph manuscripts, in-
cluding one (Vat. 3196) which was a working copy. His observations on
Petrarca's laborious revisions are exemplary both of Bembo's critical attitudes
and of a central problem in the study of the *Rime.*

13. *Rime* I, 1–2: "You who hear in scattered rimes the sound of those
sighs with which I nourished my heart." The final version reads *"Voi*
ch'ascoltate in rime sparse il suono/ di quei sospiri ond'io nudriva 'l core."

advice, will be able to say that in choosing words, which as I said is one of the basic parts of writing, he is a better composer of prose or verse and is worthy of more praise than those who take less care, when through comparison with them he finds it so.

"There are as many and even more other things to be considered, messer Ercole, in the disposition of words, as it is a much broader part than the first. For the choice is made most often in comparing one word with another or two others, whereas in order to make a good disposition of words not only is it necessary frequently to compare one word with another, but also the task is usually to compose and balance out many guises of expression with many others. Thus I say that it is like the case of the builders of the ships you have seen constructed in various areas of this city: they do three principal things. First, they look at which wood, which metal, which rope they are going to put together with which other wood, or metal, or rope—that is, in what order they are going to gather or join them together. Next, they consider that same piece of wood, which they have put together with another piece of wood or metal or rope, in order to figure out how to place it well, whether lengthwise or crosswise or inclined or upright or crooked or straight or in whatever other way. Finally, if these ropes or pieces of iron or wood are too long, they cut them to length, or if short they lengthen them, and so too they enlarge them or trim them, or in other ways taking from them or adding to them they settle them up so that the ship is composed rightly and well, as you see. So then similarly writers, too, have three parts in the disposition of their composite elements.[14] Because their first care is to see to the order, and which word to string together with which

14. Cf. Quintilian, *Instit. Orat.*, IX, iv, 146–147.

other word, that is, which verb with which noun, or else which of one or which of another part with what part of speech may be joined and composed well. After this, they have to consider these same parts and how they may be better or more beautifully put in one way than in another: that is, to consider how and in what way that word called the noun may be more charming, whether in the singular or plural, the masculine or feminine form, in the direct or oblique case; and similarly with the verb, whether it sounds better in the present or future, put in the active or passive or in any other way; and in the same way they have to consider all the other members of our speech, as much as is possible and as their quality allows. There then remains their last labor: when any of these parts, whether briefly or lengthily or otherwise disposed, seems to be without charm or without harmony, they must augment or diminish it, change or transpose it, however it may be, whether little or much, whether at the beginning or in the middle or at the end. And now if I, messer Ercole, am going to tell you, or rather to school your ears once again in those minute details appropriate to be heard by a most learned poet, and already once heard by you as a schoolboy studying Latin, then take the fault on yourself, for you desired it thus."

"And if it does not weigh too much on you," replied Strozzi, "that I give you the trouble to tell us these very minute details, messer Carlo, then as you say, 'Don't worry about me'; for as I am a master of nothing, so in these things I am truly a disciple. And nonetheless, it is the task of whoever desires to learn any discipline to begin with its principles, which are for the most part all weak and unburdensome. If I have heard another time, in doing my first works in Latin, of these same things which are said or about to be said, it will be all the better for me, for I will more easily learn it and retain the vernacular, in case I shall ever think of using it. So then, please go ahead, and do not keep quiet about anything over any part in any respect."

"If I were not to do it willingly," replied my brother, "I would go to little effort and you, messer Ercole, could get little value from it. Let us continue, then. And so that what I say be made clearer, let us talk by way of examples. Petrarca could have written the first verse of the poem which Giuliano mentioned in this way: *'Voi ch'in rime ascoltate.'* But after considering that this word *'ascoltate'* is a very lofty and clear word with its many consonants and its number of syllables and in the quality of its vowels, whereas *'rime'* for the opposite reasons is an unpretentious and less assertive word, he saw that if he said *'Voi ch'in rime'* the verse would be inclined and falling off for too long, but in saying *'Voi ch'ascoltate,'* he quickly raised it up, thus increasing its dignity. Furthermore, *'rime'* is a light and easy word, placed between the other two *'ascoltate'* and *'sparse,'* both of which are full and weighty; thus *'rime'* seems to be of both the one and the other temper. Also, it comes about in all these words recited and written in this way, *'Voi ch'ascoltate in rime sparse,'* both that they go together in a more orderly fashion and also that the vowels create a sweeter and more pleasant variety than in that other way. For these reasons it was better said as he wrote it, than if he had said it otherwise. This can serve as a cautionary example of the ordering, first of the three parts I spoke of.

"Petrarca could also have written that other verse of the same poem like this: *'Fra la vana speranza e 'l van dolore.'*[15] But because the continuing of the vowel *a* detracted from the elegance of the verse, and the variation of *e* substituted

---

15. *Rime* I, 6: "Between vain hope and vain sadness." As Bembo observes, the accepted reading is "vain hopes."

instead puts it back again, he changed the number of the less to that of the more, and made it '*Fra le vane speranze*'; and he did well, for however minor the change may be, the consequent difference is not small in elegance for all that, if one consider and think of it subtly. And this falls into the second mode of disposition mentioned above.

The third mode of disposition is the taking away of some parts from words or adding or modifying them as the case may be, as in the following example:[16]

> *Quand'era in parte altr'uom da quel ch'i sono*
> (When I was in part another man from what I am)

and this one:[17]

> *Ma ben veggi' or, sì come al popol tutto*
> *favola fui gran tempo.*
> (But now I see well how to everyone
> I was for long a fable.)

'*Uomo*' and '*popolo*' were the complete words from which he took their final vowels, and if he had not taken them away, the words would have been as languid and falling as they are now gay and courtly. It happens likewise with many others, for example,[18]

> *Che m'hanno congiurato a torto incontra*
> (Who have conspired wrongly against me)

where the poet said '*incontra*' instead of '*contra.*' And he used '*sface*' many times, and '*sevri*' frequently, and '*adiviene*' and '*dipartìo,*' instead of '*disface*' and '*separi*' and '*aviene*' and '*dipartì,*' and so too '*diemme*' and '*aprilla*' where he should correctly have said '*mi diè*' and '*la aprì.*' And although I have gathered examples of these modes of disposition from

16. *Rime* I, 4.
17. *Rime* I, 9–10.
18. *Rime* LVII, 11.

poetry, it is not the case that they do not also occur in prose. It is true that this last of the three manners comes about more rarely in prose since one deals much less with force and license of expression in prose, which does not fall under the rule of rhyme or quantity and can wander and roam about at will.

"Now as these figures have to do with syllables and single words, so I say that they pertain equally to extended constructions, and perchance all the more so. Because not every part which is completed with several words agrees with each other part, and will be better put before than after, or vice versa; and in addition, that same part does not succeed with equal grace when placed in each possible place; and if some of it is taken away or added or changed, it will result in incomparably more pleasure than otherwise; so it happens also that reasoning at length with those same figures can be much more effective than a single word. So too the discursive construction is capable of many other figures, of which the single word is not capable. This one sees clearly in the books of those who write point by point about the art of speaking. He then who pays attention to all these things, messer Ercole, when he wishes to judge two writers, whether of prose or of poetry, will perchance not be deceived, although I have not gathered together every precise detail here of those which instruct us in this matter."

BIBLIOGRAPHY
of Books and Articles in English

1. Hans Baron, *Humanistic and Political Literature in Florence and Venice at the Beginning of the Quattrocento* (reissued, New York: Russell & Russell, 1968).
2. Hans Baron, *The Crisis of the Early Italian Renaissance* (rev. 1-vol. ed., Princeton, N.J.: Princeton University Press, 1966).
3. Hans Baron, *From Petrarch to Leonardo Bruni* (Chicago and London: University of Chicago Press, 1968).
4. Cecil Grayson, "Dante in the Renaissance," in *Italian Studies Presented to E. R. Vincent* (Cambridge: Heffer, 1962), pp. 56–75. This volume also contains an article of related interest, by Frederick May, on "Ugo Foscolo's 'Parallel Between Dante and Petrarch' in Two Literary Periodicals of 1821" (pp. 219–225).
5. Cecil Grayson, "Lorenzo, Machiavelli and the Italian Language," in *Italian Renaissance Studies,* ed. E. F. Jacob (London: Faber & Faber, 1960), pp. 410–432.
6. Cecil Grayson, *A Renaissance Controversy: Latin or Italian?,* Inaugural Lecture (Oxford: Clarendon Press, 1960).
7. Revilo P. Oliver, "Petrarch's Prestige as a Humanist," in *Classical Studies in Honor of W. A. Oldfather* (Urbana, Ill.: University of Illinois Press, 1943), pp. 134–153.
8. Revilo P. Oliver, "Salutati's Criticism of Petrarch," *Italica,* 16 (1939), 49–57.
9. Jerrold E. Seigel, " 'Civic Humanism' or Ciceronian Rhetoric?", *Past and Present,* 34 (July, 1966), 3–48. For Hans Baron's reply, see *Past and Present,* 36 (April, 1967), 21–37.
10. Jerrold E. Seigel, *Rhetoric and Philosophy in Renaissance Humanism* (Princeton, N.J.: Princeton University Press, 1968).

11. David Thompson, "Landino's Life of Dante," *Dante Studies,* 88 (1970) , 119–127.

12. David Thompson, "Pico della Mirandola's Praise of Lorenzo (and Critique of Dante and Petrarch) ," *Neophilologus,* 54 (1970) , 123–126.

13. Ronald Witt, "Humanism and Rhetoric," *Il Pensiero Politico,* II, no. 1 (1969) , 75–78 (an assessment of Seigel's book) .

14. Ronald Witt, "The *De Tyranno* and Coluccio Salutati's View of Politics and Roman History," *Nuova Rivista Storica,* 53 (1969) , 434–474.

INDEX

hARpER ✦ tORChbOOKs

American Studies: General

HENRY ADAMS Degradation of the Democratic Dogma. ‡ Introduction by Charles Hirschfeld.	TB/1450

LOUIS D. BRANDEIS: Other People's Money, and How the Bankers Use It. Ed. with Intro. by Richard M. Abrams	TB/3081

HENRY STEELE COMMAGER, Ed.: The Struggle for Racial Equality	TB/1300

CARL N. DEGLER: Out of Our Past: The Forces that Shaped Modern America	CN/2

CARL N. DEGLER, Ed.: Pivotal Interpretations of American History
Vol. I TB/1240; Vol. II TB/1241

LAWRENCE H. FUCHS, Ed.: American Ethnic Politics	TB/1368

ROBERT L. HEILBRONER: The Limits of American Capitalism	TB/1305

JOHN HIGHAM, Ed.: The Reconstruction of American History	TB/1068

ROBERT H. JACKSON: The Supreme Court in the American System of Government	TB/1106

JOHN F. KENNEDY: A Nation of Immigrants. Illus. Revised and Enlarged. Introduction by Robert F. Kennedy	TB/1118

RICHARD B. MORRIS: Fair Trial: Fourteen Who Stood Accused, from Anne Hutchinson to Alger Hiss	TB/1335

GUNNAR MYRDAL: An American Dilemma: The Negro Problem and Modern Democracy. Introduction by the Author.
Vol. I TB/1443; Vol. II TB/1444

GILBERT OSOFSKY, Ed.: The Burden of Race: A Documentary History of Negro-White Relations in America	TB/1405

ARNOLD ROSE: The Negro in America: The Condensed Version of Gunnar Myrdal's An American Dilemma. Second Edition	TB/3048

JOHN E. SMITH: Themes in American Philosophy: Purpose, Experience and Community	TB/1466

WILLIAM R. TAYLOR: Cavalier and Yankee: The Old South and American National Character	TB/1474

American Studies: Colonial

BERNARD BAILYN: The New England Merchants in the Seventeenth Century	TB/1149

ROBERT E. BROWN: Middle-Class Democracy and Revolution in Massachusetts, 1691–1780. New Introduction by Author	TB/1413

JOSEPH CHARLES: The Origins of the American Party System	TB/1049

WESLEY FRANK CRAVEN: The Colonies in Transition: 1660–1712†	TB/3084

CHARLES GIBSON: Spain in America †	TB/3077

CHARLES GIBSON, Ed.: The Spanish Tradition in America +	HR/1351

LAWRENCE HENRY GIPSON: The Coming of the Revolution: 1763–1775. † Illus.	TB/3007

JACK P. GREENE, Ed.: Great Britain and the American Colonies: 1606–1763. + Introduction by the Author	HR/1477

AUBREY C. LAND, Ed.: Bases of the Plantation Society +	HR/1429

PERRY MILLER: Errand Into the Wilderness	TB/1139

PERRY MILLER & T. H. JOHNSON, Ed.: The Puritans: A Sourcebook of Their Writings
Vol. I TB/1093; Vol. II TB/1094

EDMUND S. MORGAN: The Puritan Family: Religion and Domestic Relations in Seventeenth Century New England	TB/1227

WALLACE NOTESTEIN: The English People on the Eve of Colonization: 1603-1630. † Illus.	TB/3006

LOUIS B. WRIGHT: The Cultural Life of the American Colonies: 1607-1763. † Illus.	TB/3005

YVES F. ZOLTVANY, Ed.: The French Tradition in America +	HR/1425

American Studies: The Revolution to 1860

JOHN R. ALDEN: The American Revolution: 1775-1783. † Illus.	TB/3011

RAY A. BILLINGTON: The Far Western Frontier: 1830-1860. † Illus.	TB/3012

STUART BRUCHEY: The Roots of American Economic Growth, 1607-1861: An Essay in Social Causation. New Introduction by the Author.	TB/1350

NOBLE E. CUNNINGHAM, JR., Ed.: The Early Republic, 1789-1828 +	HR/1394

GEORGE DANGERFIELD: The Awakening of American Nationalism, 1815-1828. † Illus.	TB/3061

† The New American Nation Series, edited by Henry Steele Commager and Richard B. Morris.
‡ American Perspectives series, edited by Bernard Wishy and William E. Leuchtenburg.
a History of Europe series, edited by J. H. Plumb.
§ The Library of Religion and Culture, edited by Benjamin Nelson.
‖ Researches in the Social, Cultural, and Behavioral Sciences, edited by Benjamin Nelson.
Σ Harper Modern Science Series, edited by James A. Newman.
° Not for sale in Canada.
+ Documentary History of the United States series, edited by Richard B. Morris.
# Documentary History of Western Civilization series, edited by Eugene C. Black and Leonard W. Levy.
∧ The Economic History of the United States series, edited by Henry David et al.
¶ European Perspectives series, edited by Eugene C. Black.
** Contemporary Essays series, edited by Leonard W. Levy.
* The Stratum Series, edited by John Hale.

American Studies: The Civil War to 1900

American Studies: The Twentieth Century

Art, Art History, Aesthetics

Asian Studies

Economics & Economic History

C. E. BLACK: The Dynamics of Modernization: *A Study in Comparative History* TB/1321
GILBERT BURCK & EDITOR OF *Fortune*: The Computer Age: *And its Potential for Management* TB/1179
SHEPARD B. CLOUGH, THOMAS MOODIE & CAROL MOODIE, Eds.: Economic History of Europe: *Twentieth Century* # HR/1388
THOMAS C. COCHRAN: The American Business System: *A Historical Perspective, 1900-1955* TB/1180
HAROLD U. FAULKNER: The Decline of Laissez Faire, 1897-1917 △ TB/1397
PAUL W. GATES: The Farmer's Age: *Agriculture, 1815-1860* △ TB/1398
WILLIAM GREENLEAF, Ed.: American Economic Development Since 1860 + HR/1353
ROBERT L. HEILBRONER: The Future as History: *The Historic Currents of Our Time and the Direction in Which They Are Taking America* TB/1386
ROBERT L. HEILBRONER: The Great Ascent: *The Struggle for Economic Development in Our Time* TB/3030
DAVID S. LANDES: Bankers and Pashas: *International Finance and Economic Imperialism in Egypt. New Preface by the Author* TB/1412
ROBERT LATOUCHE: The Birth of Western Economy: *Economic Aspects of the Dark Ages* TB/1290
W. ARTHUR LEWIS: The Principles of Economic Planning. *New Introduction by the Author*° TB/1436
ROBERT GREEN MC CLOSKEY: American Conservatism in the Age of Enterprise TB/1137
WILLIAM MILLER, Ed.: Men in Business: *Essays on the Historical Role of the Entrepreneur* TB/1081
HERBERT A. SIMON: The Shape of Automation: *For Men and Management* TB/1245

Historiography and History of Ideas

J. BRONOWSKI & BRUCE MAZLISH: The Western Intellectual Tradition: *From Leonardo to Hegel* TB/3001
WILHELM DILTHEY: Pattern and Meaning in History: *Thoughts on History and Society.*° *Edited with an Intro. by H. P. Rickman* TB/1075
J. H. HEXTER: More's Utopia: *The Biography of an Idea. Epilogue by the Author* TB/1195
H. STUART HUGHES: History as Art and as Science: *Twin Vistas on the Past* TB/1207
ARTHUR O. LOVEJOY: The Great Chain of Being: *A Study of the History of an Idea* TB/1009
RICHARD H. POPKIN: The History of Scenticism from Erasmus to Descartes. *Revised Edition* TB/1391
MASSIMO SALVADORI, Ed.: Modern Socialism # HR/1374
BRUNO SNELL: The Discovery of the Mind: *The Greek Origins of European Thought* TB/1018

History: General

HANS KOHN: The Age of Nationalism: *The First Era of Global History* TB/1380
BERNARD LEWIS: The Arabs in History TB/1029
BERNARD LEWIS: The Middle East and the West ° TB/1274

History: Ancient

A. ANDREWS: The Greek Tyrants TB/1103

THEODOR H. GASTER: Thespis: *Ritual Myth and Drama in the Ancient Near East* TB/1281
MICHAEL GRANT: Ancient History ° TB/1190

History: Medieval

NORMAN COHN: The Pursuit of the Millennium: *Revolutionary Messianism in Medieval and Reformation Europe* TB/1037
F. L. GANSHOF: Feudalism TB/1058
F. L. GANSHOF: The Middle Ages: *A History of International Relations. Translated by Rémy Hall* TB/1411
ROBERT LATOUCHE: The Birth of Western Economy: *Economic Aspects of the Dark Ages* ° TB/1290
HENRY CHARLES LEA: The Inquisition of the Middle Ages. || *Introduction by Walter Ullmann* TB/1456

History: Renaissance & Reformation

JACOB BURCKHARDT: The Civilization of the Renaissance in Italy. *Introduction by Benjamin Nelson and Charles Trinkaus. Illus.* Vol. I TB/40; Vol. II TB/41
JOHN CALVIN & JACOPO SADOLETO: A Reformation Debate. *Edited by John C. Olin* TB/1239
FEDERICO CHABOD: Machiavelli and the Renaissance TB/1193
THOMAS CROMWELL: Thomas Cromwell: *Selected Letters on Church and Commonwealth, 1523-1540. ¶ Ed. with an Intro. by Arthur J. Slavin* TB/1462
FRANCESCO GUICCIARDINI: History of Florence. *Translated with an Introduction and Notes by Mario Domandi* TB/1470
WERNER L. GUNDERSHEIMER, Ed.: French Humanism, 1470-1600. * Illus.* TB/1473
HANS J. HILLERBRAND, Ed., The Protestant Reformation # HR/1342
JOHAN HUIZINGA: Erasmus and the Age of Reformation. *Illus.* TB/19
JOEL HURSTFIELD: The Elizabethan Nation TB/1312
JOEL HURSTFIELD, Ed.: The Reformation Crisis TB/1267
PAUL OSKAR KRISTELLER: Renaissance Thought: *The Classic, Scholastic, and Humanist Strains* TB/1048
PAUL OSKAR KRISTELLER: Renaissance Thought II: *Papers on Humanism and the Arts* TB/1163
PAUL O. KRISTELLER & PHILIP P. WIENER, Eds.: Renaissance Essays TB/1392
DAVID LITTLE: Religion, Order and Law: *A Study in Pre-Revolutionary England. § Preface by R. Bellah* TB/1418
NICCOLO MACHIAVELLI: History of Florence and of the Affairs of Italy: *From the Earliest Times to the Death of Lorenzo the Magnificent. Introduction by Felix Gilbert* TB/1027
ALFRED VON MARTIN: Sociology of the Renaissance. ° *Introduction by W. K. Ferguson* TB/1099
GARRETT MATTINGLY et al.: Renaissance Profiles. *Edited by J. H. Plumb* TB/1162
J. H. PARRY: The Establishment of the European Hegemony: 1415-1715: *Trade and Exploration in the Age of the Renaissance* TB/1045
PAOLO ROSSI: Philosophy, Technology, and the Arts, in the Early Modern Era 1400-1700. || *Edited by Benjamin Nelson. Translated by Salvator Attanasio* TB/1458
R. H. TAWNEY: The Agrarian Problem in the Sixteenth Century. *Intro. by Lawrence Stone* TB/1315

H. R. TREVOR-ROPER: The European Witch-craze of the Sixteenth and Seventeenth Centuries and Other Essays ° TB/1416

VESPASIANO: Rennaissance Princes, Popes, and XVth Century: The Vespasiano Memoirs. Introduction by Myron P. Gilmore. Illus. TB/1111

History: Modern European

MAX BELOFF: The Age of Absolutism, 1660-1815 TB/1062

D. W. BROGAN: The Development of Modern France ° Vol. I: From the Fall of the Empire to the Dreyfus Affair TB/1184 Vol. II: The Shadow of War, World War I, Between the Two Wars TB/1185

ALAN BULLOCK: Hitler, A Study in Tyranny. ° Revised Edition. Illus. TB/1123

JOHANN GOTTLIEB FICHTE: Addresses to the German Nation. Ed. with Intro. by George A. Kelly ¶ TB/1366

ALBERT GOODWIN: The French Revolution TB/1064

H. STUART HUGHES: The Obstructed Path: French Social Thought in the Years of Desperation TB/1451

JOHAN HUIZINGA: Dutch Civilization in the 17th Century and Other Essays TB/1453

JOHN MCMANNERS: European History, 1789-1914: Men, Machines and Freedom TB/1419

FRANZ NEUMANN: Behemoth: The Structure and Practice of National Socialism, 1933-1944 TB/1289

DAVID OGG: Europe of the Ancien Régime, 1715-1783 ° α TB/1271

ALBERT SOREL: Europe Under the Old Regime. Translated by Francis H. Herrick TB/1121

A. J. P. TAYLOR: From Napoleon to Lenin: Historical Essays ° TB/1268

A. J. P. TAYLOR: The Habsburg Monarchy, 1809-1918: A History of the Austrian Empire and Austria-Hungary ° TB/1187

J. M. THOMPSON: European History, 1494-1789 TB/1431

H. R. TREVOR-ROPER: Historical Essays TB/1269

Literature & Literary Criticism

JACQUES BARZUN: The House of Intellect TB/1051

W. J. BATE: From Classic to Romantic: Premises of Taste in Eighteenth Century England TB/1036

VAN WYCK BROOKS: Van Wyck Brooks: The Early Years: A Selection from his Works, 1908-1921 Ed. with Intro. by Claire Sprague TB/3082

RICHMOND LATTIMORE, Translator: The Odyssey of Homer TB/1389

Philosophy

HENRI BERGSON: Time and Free Will: An Essay on the Immediate Data of Consciousness ° TB/1021

H. J. BLACKHAM: Six Existentialist Thinkers: Kierkegaard, Nietzsche, Jaspers, Marcel, Heidegger, Sartre ° TB/1002

J. M. BOCHENSKI: The Methods of Contemporary Thought. Trans by Peter Caws TB/1377

CRANE BRINTON: Nietzsche. Preface, Bibliography, and Epilogue by the Author TB/1197

ERNST CASSIRER: Rousseau, Kant and Goethe. Intro by Peter Gay TB/1092

WILFRID DESAN: The Tragic Finale: An Essay on the Philosophy of Jean-Paul Sartre TB/1030

MARVIN FARBER: The Aims of Phenomenology: The Motives, Methods, and Impact of Husserl's Thought TB/1291

PAUL FRIEDLANDER: Plato: An Introduction TB/2017

MICHAEL GELVEN: A Commentary on Heidegger's "Being and Time" TB/1464

G. W. F. HEGEL: On Art, Religion Philosophy: Introductory Lectures to the Realm of Absolute Spirit. ‖ Edited with an Introduction by J. Glenn Gray TB/1463

G. W. F. HEGEL: Phenomenology of Mind. ° ‖ Introduction by eGorge Lichtheim TB/1303

MARTIN HEIDEGGER: Discourse on Thinking. Translated with a Preface by John M. Anderson and E. Hans Freund. Introduction by John M. Anderson TB/1459

F. H. HEINEMANN: Existentialism and the Modern Predicament TB/28

WERER HEISENBERG: Physics and Philosophy: The Revolution in Modern Science. Intro. by F. S. C. Northrop TB/549

EDMUND HUSSERL: Phenomenology and the Crisis of Philosophy. § Translated with an Introduction by Quentin Lauer TB/1170

IMMANUEL KANT: Groundwork of the Metaphysic of Morals. Translated and Analyzed by H. J. Paton TB/1159

IMMANUEL KANT: Lectures on Ethics. § Introduction by Lewis White Beck TB/105

QUENTIN LAUER: Phenomenology: Its Genesis and Prospect. Preface by Aron Gurwitsch TB/1169

GEORGE A. MORGAN: What Nietzsche Means TB/1198

H. J. PATON: The Categorical Imperative: A Study in Kant's Moral Philosophy TB/1325

MICHAEL POLANYI: Personal Knowledge: Towards a Post-Critical Philosophy TB/1158

WILLARD VAN ORMAN QUINE: Elementary Logic Revised Edition TB/577

JOHN E. SMITH: Themes in American Philosophy: Purpose, Experience and Community TB/1466

MORTON WHITE: Foundations of Historical Knowledge TB/1440

WILHELM WINDELBAND: A History of Philosophy Vol. I: Greek, Roman, Medieval TB/38 Vol. II: Renaissance, Enlightenment, Modern TB/39

LUDWIG WITTGENSTEIN: The Blue and Brown Books ° TB/1211

LUDWIG WITTGENSTEIN: Notebooks, 1914-1916 TB/1441

Political Science & Government

C. E. BLACK: The Dynamics of Modernization: A Study in Comparative History TB/1321

KENNETH E. BOULDING: Conflict and Defense: A General Theory of Action TB/3024

DENIS W. BROGAN: Politics in America. New Introduction by the Author TB/1469

LEWIS COSER, Ed.: Political Sociology TB/1293

ROBERT A. DAHL & CHARLES E. LINDBLOM: Politics, Economics, and Welfare: Planning and Politico-Economic Systems Resolved into Basic Social Processes TB/3037

ROY C. MACRIDIS, Ed.: Political Parties: Contemporary Trends and Ideas ** TB/1322

ROBERT GREEN MC CLOSKEY: American Conservatism in the Age of Enterprise, 1865-1910 TB/1137

JOHN B. MORRALL: Political Thought in Medieval Times TB/1076

71 72 73 74   12 11 10 9 8 7 6 5 4 3 2 1